Coherent Christianity

Louis Roy

Coherent Christianity

NOVALIS

© 2005 Novalis, Saint Paul University, Ottawa, Canada

Cover design: Audrey Wells
Layout: Caroline Galhidi

Business Office:
Novalis
49 Front Street East, 2nd Floor
Toronto, Ontario, Canada
M5E 1B3

Phone: 1-800-387-7164
Fax: 1-800-204-4140
E-mail: cservice@novalis-inc.com
www.novalis.ca

Library and Archives Canada Cataloguing in Publication

Roy, Louis, 1942–
    Coherent Christianity / Louis Roy.

Translation of: La foi en quête de cohérence. (Les Éditions Bellarmin, 1988)
Includes bibliographical references.
ISBN 2-89507-375-9

    1. Faith. 2. Experience (Religion). 3. Christianity. 4. Religion and
culture. I. Title.

BT771.2.R6713 2005   234'.2   C2005-904687-2

Printed in Canada.

We acknowledge the financial support of the Government of Canada through the Book Publishing Industry
Development Program (BPIDP) for our publishing activities.

5 4 3 2 1   09 08 07 06 05

Contents

Introduction 7

Part I: Overview
   1. A Real-life Adventure 12
   2. The Components of Christian Experience 22

Part II: Relationship with God
   3. The Act of Christian Faith 40
   4. Ideologies and Disillusionment 49
   5. Religious Reasons to Hope 56
   6. Human Desire and Love of God 64

Part III: Pastoral Discernment
   7. Three Mentalities Faced by the Churches 82
   8. Evoking, Discerning, and Extending the Experience .. 87
   9. Interiority and Relationality 92
   10. The Gospel and Everyday Life 103

Part IV: Critical Dialogue
   11. On Reincarnation 116
   12. The Words of a Spiritual Master 123
   13. Bernard Lonergan: A Theologian in Dialogue 134

Conclusion 140
Notes 141

Introduction

Through this book, I hope to express my conviction that Christianity offers the deepest experience to which human beings are invited by God. The Christian experience involves meaning and truth, hope and love, suffering and joy. It is a myriad of diverse paths, travelled by people of all classes and races. It is a space of freedom, where each person must seek the light and make their decisions, interacting with the intellectual and affective resources of their culture. Because the Christian experience is also one of solidarity, I offer here, as a believer and a theologian, some clarifications and interpretations that I hope will serve as beacons along the way.

Over the years, numerous readers have told me how much they appreciated my articles. This was an incentive for me to present my convictions in the form of a book: I hope thus to reach other readers for whom religious faith is real and who wish to achieve greater intellectual integrity. Indeed, the aim of the reflections you will find in these pages is to foster a gradual integration of the various dimensions that make up our human and Christian lived experience. I am thinking of those people and places involved in the search for the meaning of life, open to spirituality and meditation, and affected by the scientific, humanist, and psychological cultures of the industrialized countries, facing the challenge of collective hope and openness to others. I am speaking to people who, like myself, ask questions, have doubts, and do their best to understand and listen to what others may have to teach them.

My intent is theological in nature. To show the underlying coherence of the Christian experience, I will present an overview, then an analysis of the dynamics of our relationship with God, and, finally, reflections on the way faith and culture interact. You will find in these pages a traditional Catholic theology, expressed in a contemporary manner thanks to Bernard Lonergan's philosophy of human intentionality, which requires knowing the self as an aware, active, loving and religious subject. This theological vision is concretely expressed in various ways: pastoral concern, dialogue with the psychologies of North American humanism and European existentialism, openness to religiosity and spirituality, and scrutiny of the meanings and values held by current western society.

Part I of this book paints a general picture of the Christian faith understood as a personal and communal adventure—a sequence of real life experiences. Here, things are not viewed objectively, as realities to be defined (although I do not in any way deny the importance of that aspect), but rather from the perspective of the seeking human subject, invited by the Gospel to make a number of discoveries. For those seeking an understanding that is at the same time flexible and in keeping with Christian truth, I have drawn a kind of road map that may help them to identify and situate the perceptions that define their faith approach. I developed this outline in Montreal, with students from the Institut de pastorale, in a workshop where we evaluated our journey of faith. Participants used it to identify the various components of the Gospel lived out in today's context and to examine the strengths and weakness of their Christian experience. I applied, revised, and gradually transformed this outline into a methodical text with these adults, aged 30 to 50. I subsequently used this text in other workshops as well as for "study days" focusing on some of the components it described. I also used it in courses whose purpose was to discuss stages of evangelization: in this context, the outline was in the form of a chart, to help spiritual guides discern what discovery might be made next by the person or group they were accompanying.

In Part II, I focus on the three fundamental attitudes that constitute our relationship with God: faith, hope and love. With respect to the act of faith, Chapter 3 analyzes the discoveries and motives that justify the amazing decision to believe not only in God, but also, while keeping a critical mind, in what the Catholic Church teaches to be true. The next two chapters deal with hope: Chapter 4 outlines a theological critique of ideologies that have led to disenchantment in the Western world, while Chapter 5 identifies the religious foundations of hope. Chapter 6 deals with the subject of love, from a psychological and philosophical perspective of human desire, showing how it affects our experience of God, the meaning of sin and our encounter with the life and teaching of Jesus.

In Part III, "Pastoral Discernment," I try to highlight what things need to be emphasized and given priority in a renewed interpretation of the Christian experience. I describe the appeals made to us by the different mentalities playing a major role in shaping our culture. I also present criteria to help facilitate spiritual discernment, pastoral companioning, liturgical symbolism, and serving the word of God.

Part IV applies the intellectual and spiritual discernment criteria to the thought of three authors: Jean-Luc Hétu, Karlfried Graf Dürckheim, and Bernard Lonergan. In my disagreement with Hétu, I dwell on the issue of the coherence and truth of Christianity in a way that complements what I write about the Christian faith in Chapter 3. The chapter on Dürckheim notes the important role of transcendent experiences, brings out the signs of religious authenticity, and pays special attention to the relationship between the experiential core that religions share and the way this core is interpreted by Christianity. In the final chapter, where I present the theologian from whom I have learned the most in terms of methodology, I point out how much religion stands to gain from dialogue with philosophy, psychology and culture. I then return to the question of the relationship between subjectivity and objectivity, which I addressed briefly in Chapter 1.

Insofar as inclusive language is concerned, I alternate masculine and feminine pronouns. However, in accordance with biblical custom, God is referred to as "he." Furthermore, in this English translation, the author has updated certain sentences.

Louis Roy, OP
Boston
May 2005

Part I

OVERVIEW

1

A Real-life Adventure

I n this chapter, I would like to present the realizations and personal convictions that brought me to the particular notion of faith underlying everything I write in this book.

An initial shock

In the spring of 1964, after two years of monastic life in France, I returned to Quebec and resumed contact with friends and former buddies from the *collège* who were at this point finishing their second year of university. What did I observe? People who had completed their Catholic classical studies in a mood of genuine religious fervour, intensified by a great seven-day retreat, were now non-practising, uncomfortable with their faith, and in some cases, agnostic. I cannot say it upset me, for I had gone through a period of faith rejection myself between the ages of 16 and 19, but it was a shock to me nevertheless. It made me ask: How is it possible that our Jesuit religious education, which was, after all, intellectually rigorous, didn't stick for more than a year in the university environment? The more I conversed with these school friends, now immersed in the study of history, literature, psychology, social work, or natural science, the better I understood that there had been a major shift in the way they looked at life.

In 1964, I was not yet aware that a "quiet revolution" was under way in Quebec. But seeing all these people in religious difficulty led me to realize that, if the Christian faith had a future, it could never again be lived the same way as before. It became clear to me that our "traditional religion"—even well explained and in part renewed—could not co-exist with the way of thinking that informed the human sciences and with the enormous amounts of information my contemporaries were absorbing. In a society undergoing rapid social and economic change, new sensibilities and mentalities were developing which the person of intellectual integrity could not reconcile with the Catholicism of their childhood—even considering its adapted liturgy, catechesis and vocabulary. Renovating the inside of the building called faith was no longer enough: we needed to rebuild from scratch, using old as well as new materials, but arranging them according to a design that honoured contemporary thinking and method.

The shock I received at the time made me keep repeating to myself, "Things can no longer stay the same." This rather vague thought has influenced my research ever since. I soon found this conviction confirmed in the Dominican journals *Témoin* [Witness] and *Maintenant* [Now], which I was reading to stay in touch with a body of thought outlining an authentic path into the future. The ideas I found there helped consolidate my impressions. My close relationship with friends who perceived the world in a new way and were posing valid questions was an equally strong factor in my intellectual evolution. As long as one maintains a safe emotional distance from those who doubt, it is easy to defend one's traditional religion—in its more or less adapted version—and to find all sorts of explanations for the lack of belief or confused belief of others. But when you are immersed in the same ascendant culture yourself, and when you have the same questions about the realities of life, you travel the road together, each seeking in your own way.

Ecclesial experience and dialogue

Following a year studying literature at Université Laval in Quebec City, my searching led me to join the Dominicans, where I saw both a desire for intellectual honesty and an openness to the tremendous and the marvellous in religious experience. I found that, despite certain intellectual and religious distortions, their questioning was rigorous and based on current philosophy. They were also making a vigorous effort to mine the Bible and centuries of Christian thought for wisdom that could nourish starving hearts and minds. During these long years of training, I lived an intense experience of church in terms not only of community but also of prayer and the sharing of questions and answers. This ecclesial experience was later expanded through my deeply moving encounter with Jean Vanier and the *Foi et partage* (Faith and Sharing) groups, then through Bethany House, where the Jesus

Prayer and the Taizé liturgies made an impression on me, and finally, through the Institut de pastorale, where I think I have been able, in dialogue with my students, to develop a theology of faith capable of reaching a good many of our contemporaries.

I must admit, however, that my study of Christian tradition and my quasi-autarkical religious life environment sometimes distanced me from my friends who were becoming increasingly removed from Catholicism. As we did not share quite the same experience, it was hard for me to understand the way they reacted and reflected, based on what they were living. I saw that people could settle into separate worlds. Perhaps I feared the part of their experience that was foreign to me, and their surprising ideas, whose source I was unfamiliar with. My insecurity sometimes led me to judge others and to sound defensive. But, because of mutual friendship, we were able to show trust and openness. I would wonder, for example, about this friend or that one: Just what is he looking for and what is making him choose that particular path? In this way, my anxious feelings of being disoriented were transformed into the beginnings of comprehension.

During all those years of dialogue, how often I had kept quiet about my religious experience, how often I had listened at length! By instinctively adapting my missionary zeal, I entered the difficult state of the witness to the Gospel who cannot offer directly to the other the hidden treasure they have discovered. Without any kind of denial on my part—for the people I talked with were perfectly aware I remained committed to life in my religious community—I experienced the frustration of talking only in discrete allusive language about this God who was so central to my life. But this frustration evaporated as soon as it dawned on me that, without giving up my practice of confronting others or raising pertinent questions, I could have confidence in the course they were on, for the Holy Spirit was at the heart of their search.

Convictions about the life of faith

I would like now to share my convictions about the life of faith. These have grown as much out of my own experience as out of my reading and my contact with others who are searching. Through my clear articulation of these convictions, you will be able to see the thinking behind the faith outline that I will present afterwards. These convictions may be expressed in four points: our current experience of the Gospel is both subjective and objective; it is both incomplete and coherent; it is both free and community-based; and it is both natural and God-given.

1. An experience that is both subjective and objective

It seems to me that in the contemporary mind there exists a demand for intellectual honesty that excludes having as one's starting point an acceptance of the Christian message without first meeting the prerequisites of searching, questioning, and religious experience. Faith can no longer be based on apologetics, even if the latter contains elements that are valid and useful in a different context. This new context no longer gives priority to proofs and truths guaranteed by authorities, but to the human subject in search of values and meaning. In my opinion, we must see faith first and foremost from a subjective viewpoint, trusting in the natural movement that goes from the subjective to the objective. While subjectivism keeps intelligence confined within its own limits, a proper understanding of subjectivity will include the notion that God created it in such a way that it strives, albeit gropingly, towards objective reality.

Revelation relies primarily on the human spirit, created by God to seek, love, know, and serve God, for it is in the human spirit that every religious discovery takes place. Certainly, it is through Jesus that we come to know the Creator in the deepest sense, but we cannot perceive Christ's radical identity and liberating role unless the Creator first enlivens in us an impulse to seek. "No one can come to me unless drawn by the Father who sent me" (John 6:44). By examining the subjective aspect of our experience, we can discern what is meant by being "drawn." In doing so, we turn our attention to how we live reality—that is to say, to the inner effect that outer events produce in us—in a way that enables us to recognize God's call in them.

2. An experience that is both incomplete and coherent

The process of living out the Gospel constantly remains incomplete, since there is always more to experience and to discover. In other words, considering all the dimensions the Gospel invites us to live, we cannot discover everything at the same time or experience everything with the same intensity. Recognizing this incomplete character of the faith of groups and individuals alike can break down the intolerance we easily harbour towards one another. Indeed, depending on our particular sensitivities, we may expect of others that they should be on an intensive quest, or should submit to church teaching, or go to Mass every Sunday, or be more involved in their community, and so forth. But what if, in the meantime, these people were bringing to fruition a different discovery from the one we had in mind for them?

A dynamic faith life does not necessarily progress in accordance with others' expectations; the order in which we make discoveries varies significantly with the individual or the group. However, over time, this kind of faith development displays amazing logic: progress in one component of the Gospel raises a problem or a question that entails a step forward in another component. One can go, for example, from love of neighbour to love of God , from seeking to community, from affective relationship to the desire to understand, or inversely. In short, it is normal that, along the religious journey, there are places where we linger, and that progress in one area leads to openness and attention to other areas. The desire for an intellectual and practical coherence draws people, according to their own rhythm, to be interested in the Gospel adventure as a whole.

3. An experience that is both free and community-based

For many centuries, no doubt ever since the era of Constantine, religion was presented in the context of authority. Today, in the context of institutional secularization, Christian churches are playing the card of religious freedom. But is it not true that very often, once an individual commits to the Good News of Jesus, we are eager to present them with a number of obligations? Do we not thus risk upsetting the rhythm of their searching and discovering? Is unconditional respect for people's freedom just as valid for those who are members of the church? Personally, I find it hard to let go of the reflex to say "one must" with respect to matters I consider important for others to know and to practise. Jesus, however, made a point of saying to the rich young man, "If you wish..." (Matt. 19:21).

What prevents so many Christians from wholeheartedly accepting their religious freedom in all matters—belief, liturgy, morality, etc.—may be fear of the insecurity that inevitably accompanies the personal act of faith. We are inclined to rely on proofs and authorities, even on efforts to impress people unduly, instead of searching out the conditions that enable us to place an enlightened trust in the church and in Jesus. On the contrary, it seems to me we can bet that an authentic personal journey will lead quite naturally to the irreplaceable tenets of the church community. Indeed, a climate of sound religious freedom leads a person to acknowledge voluntarily the role that individuals and groups have played in his or her religious development. The message and spirit of Jesus have been handed down through a historical line of similar witnesses. Thus, when the perspectives revealed to us upon discovering Jesus are freely accepted, the decision to conform our life to the word of God is made in solidarity with our Christian sisters and brothers.

4. An experience that is both natural and God-given

Finally, I want to identify a fourth characteristic of the Christian faith, the seed of which is found in the other three: the naturalness of the Gospel experience which brings into play our real lives and the way that human beings actually function. Our encounter with God is always mediated by the deeper level of our lives. Revelation makes its way right through our entire being—heart, mind, soul, and body—so that this clay enriched by grace will be worth cultivating. Nothing is ever gained by pushing aside the events, questions, feelings, and intuitions that arise in life. The Holy Spirit, the One who is our help in all circumstances, uses these natural elements to lead us gradually to discover the various aspects of faith. The Gospel experience would still not be possible if God were not supporting us by guiding our intelligence and stimulating our progress; what is more, the Gospel experience would not be an experience *of* God if he were not freely giving himself to us in it.

This conviction that the Holy Spirit both respects and at the same time activates the human process, enables the "evangelizing" person to give serious attention to others' lived experience, and to have great patience with what might appear to be a slow pace, or even stagnation or regression. In this human-divine adventure, Christian witnesses and guides can only exercise a subordinate role, leaving the work of salvation to "God our Saviour, who desires everyone to be saved and to come to the knowledge of the truth" (1 Tim. 2:4).

The tree of faith

The convictions I have just described and the components of Christian experience that I have identified gave me the idea of using the image of a tree to illustrate the progress of faith. This tree represents the human subject, growing from a single seed biologically programmed to become a tree, incomplete in its development but striving towards a comprehensive design, possessing its individual traits even as its branches reach outward to create communities and societies with others, able to depend on its own inner resources as well as the resources it gets from its immediate environment: earth, air, rain, and sun.

The image of the tree recurs numerous times in the Bible to designate the believer to whom God promises fulfillment. The best-known example from the Hebrew Scriptures is the first psalm (see also Psalm 52:10); but I will quote instead a parallel passage from Jeremiah:

> Blessed are those who trust in the Lord,
> whose trust is in the Lord.
> They shall be like a tree planted by water,
> sending out its roots by the stream.
> It shall not fear when heat comes,
> and its leaves shall stay green;
> in the year of drought it is not anxious,
> and it does not cease to bear fruit. (Jer. 17:7-8)

For his part, Hosea compares the people of Israel, loved by God, to a solid oak and to a splendid olive tree (Hos.14:6-7). In the book of Ben Sirach, Wisdom declares, as she sings her own praises, that she grew tall in Zion like a cedar, a cypress, a palm tree (Sir. 24:12-22). If we understand these verses as a prefiguration of Jesus, we can consider him the model tree with respect to growth as well as fruit.

Jesus himself, moreover, made a comparison between the reign he was announcing and the incredible development of a tree from a tiny seed:

> The kingdom of heaven is like a mustard seed that someone took and sowed in his field; it is the smallest of all the seeds, but when it has grown it is the greatest of shrubs and becomes a tree, so that the birds of the air come and make nests in its branches. (Matt. 13:31-32)

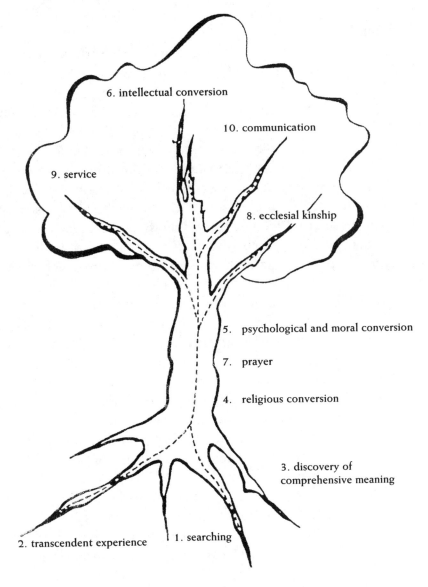

As for the parable of the barren fig tree, the severity of the Marcan (11:12–14:21-22) and Matthean (21:18-22) versions suggests a lesson on dried up religion and on living faith. But the Lucan version is more relevant to our topic: there, the gardener expresses hope for this tree. "Sir, let it alone for one more year, until I dig around it and put manure on it. If it bears fruit next year, well and good; but if not, you can cut it down" (Luke 13:8-9; see 6-9). We are warned about the possibility of being a useless tree or even a harmful one (it is "wasting the soil"), but we are also told of the Saviour's concern for our growth and our fruitfulness.

Let us look now at the tree of faith and see how the various aspects of life lived according to the Gospel may be expressed as components of it.

First of all, our searching (1) constitutes the soil in which the word of God is planted and begins to grow. This search includes, on the one hand, our aspirations towards values that draw us beyond our achievements and our limits and, on the other hand, our quest for ultimate meaning in our lives. Two kinds of roots develop in this compost: transcendent experiences (2), in which the person comes up against something totally surpassing them and perceives that they are in connection, particularly affective connection, with a unique Reality; discovery of comprehensive meaning (3), in which the person glimpses that a meaningful life is possible, that their path and that of others may be directed towards a mysterious destiny.

These first three components of the Christian experience make up God's three-fold call: through the capacity to seek God, which we received from God when God created us, and through that warmth and light which surge within us, in the experience of transcendence, on the one hand, and in the discovery of comprehensive meaning, on the other. Warmth and light draw us towards that Fire that enlivens our emotions and enlightens our minds. As for the response we can give, it is both inner—the three conversions and prayer—and outer—kinship, service and communication.

There are three conversions at the centre of the Gospel experience and these constitute the trunk of the tree. Religious conversion (4) is acceptance of the fact of being in relationship with God, whether we refer to God in confessional language or intuit God as Meaning, Love,

Life, etc. Psychological and moral conversion (5) is the equivalent of entering into a process of gradual purification of our relationship with ourselves, others and the world. Intellectual conversion (6) is located at the top of the tree, for there we acquire that comprehensive view, the true Gospel perspective on people and things. Finally, prayer (7) completes the inner response to God's call, in that it is the conscious renewal of the three conversions and it is the dialogue with God that runs through all the other components of Christian experience. I compare prayer with the sap that runs through the entire tree: roots, trunk, and branches.

The last three dimensions express our relationship to others and to the world. These are the branches that connect with those of other trees, creating wooded spaces where people can organize their collective existence; these branches bear leaves, flowers and fruits, signalling pure gift as well as usefulness. Ecclesial kinship (8) translates a deep interpersonal solidarity as sisters and brothers, both in our humanity and in our destiny, and as daughters and sons of one Creator. Service (9) designates that great work that strives to encourage life in nature and matter, at home as well as at work, and within the complex economic, social and political institutions that govern our inter-human relationships.Finally, communication (10) seeks to share the searching, the experience, and the wisdom.

2

The Components of Christian Experience

The following components of Christian experience are the constitutive elements of a life lived in accordance with the Gospel today. The order in which they are presented is not chronological, but that of a person on a journey who moves by stages from a place of searching to one of communicating her faith. Many other itineraries are also possible starting from any component, for each one opens onto the Christian mystery. Like the chemical elements of a body, the various components of the contemporary experience of the Gospel cannot be separated from one another: they are interdependent and exist in mutual complementarity. All these aspects taken together constitute a complete structure of the Christian life, which can be used to assess one's faith or to help others grow in discovering and practising the Gospel. While I am presenting these categories in a Christian context, they describe a type of experience that also takes place in other great religions as well as in secular contexts.

1. Searching

Searching represents the soil in which God's call can reach a human being. This call can only be perceived by a searching person, that is, one who is open to something other than what is offered to her by her everyday life. And yet it is in everyday life that this openness or this searching takes place. Everyday life experience is permeated by a fundamental search, which rests on two pillars.

The first pillar supporting this search is all of a person's deepest aspirations: her needs, hopes, desires; her search for love, justice, individual or collective liberation; and her pursuit of values, her efforts and her projects.

The second pillar supporting this searching is the quest for meaning, that is, this mental reflex we have of seeking the meaning of what we are living. Why is this particular thing happening to me? What is the significance of this or that event for me? What was my motive in choosing this thing over that one? For what reason did I join this group, or commit to that project? Why do I devote time and energy to certain types of activities?

Our two-fold search—through our aspirations and our quest for meaning—marks our everyday life experience. It enlivens the most banal and the most profound of our human experiences. The banality, for example, of our eat-work-sleep routine calls into question our aspirations and our quest for meaning: Am I satisfied with this? Does this make any sense? Could I live this in a more human way? On the other hand, our more conscious experiences, such as the search for our identity, loneliness, the suffering caused by failure, short or long bouts of illness, intense joy, communication and intimacy, the ambiguity of values not fully lived out, aging and the certainty of death—all of these send us back to our basic hopes and our need for meaning.

In this soil of our radical search, of our either ardent or half-hearted yearning to be fulfilled human beings, God too seeks us. We can, however, run away from God or from ourselves by being resigned, stifling our aspirations, and dismissing valid and pertinent questions about the meaning and direction of our lives. Unfortunately, it is possible to cling to routines and ready-made answers, which prevent us from seeing in our concrete existence the emptiness that only the Infinite One can fill. Thinking to protect ourselves against that which would stand in the way of our living, we sometimes refuse that which would enable us to live fully.

In other words, our search is both sincere and handicapped, for, while we may long for happiness and human fulfillment, our weakness and the dizzying pace of the daily round tend to make us skeptical about achieving them.

2. Transcendent experience

Every person's life is normally marked by several transcendent experiences, that is to say, events that strike us with a certain intensity and give us a glimpse of something great that is beyond us. We have no doubt more than once recognized the presence of God in nature, in solitary reflection, in a community celebration, or in life's trials. For some years now, "personalism" has emphasized finding God in others; it is true that the mystery of a person opens us to an order of reality that commands our absolute respect and admiration. What we may not be sufficiently aware of is that there are myriad other occasions of religious experience to which we hardly pay attention because we tend to think of them as purely natural or secular, but which are no less important as ways in which God reveals himself to us.

Every dense human experience thus becomes a place of religious experience insofar as it leads us to feel that we are open to something that is absolutely beyond us. We are indeed talking about a feeling—intense or moderate, as the case may be—for it is our deep emotions that are affected; but this feeling is the vehicle for a perception that can be expressed as intuitive knowledge. It seems that most transcendent experiences remain unexpressed, but if we could identify such experiences in ourselves, we could more easily discover who our personal God is and truly rejoice at having really met this God. In fact, I am convinced that through these natural events God gives us the grace of divine connection. From a phenomenological perspective, the feeling shows only that the heart is open to something more than what the naked eye can see. Moreover, psychologists interpret this openness in various ways. From a faith perspective, we can say that God offers his love and light to whoever lives this experience, as long as it is morally good.

Human events that are virtually places of religious experience are dense human experiences, like fields of our lived experience that are ploughed up by our aspirations and our quest for meaning. Whether it is happy or sad, more positive or more negative, this lived experience is then unexpectedly permeated by a unique atmosphere, in which we experience either the power and beauty of a reality; the steadfastness of the Being in whom our life is anchored; the attraction of a particular value; or communion with an incomparable Presence. Whichever of these four types it belongs to—aesthetic, ontological, ethical, or interpersonal—and whether you call it religious experience, experience of the sacred, a peak experience, or an experience of Being or of Transcendence, this experience is valid in itself and fosters the emergence of comprehensive meaning. Its long-term effects are ambiguous, however, for it can just as easily lead the individual or the group to withdraw into a wrongly oriented spirituality as lead them to intensify their daily efforts and their involvement in their community.

3. The discovery of comprehensive meaning

Immersed in their daily affairs, people rarely reflect explicitly on the ultimate or comprehensive meaning of their existence. What pre-occupies us is the simple meaning of our day-to-day actions; also, the meaning of a project, of a period in our life, or of an unusual or typical event that makes us question our routine or which, on the contrary, sums up and expresses the orientation of our everyday life; or else it is collective meaning, which can be found in or brought to a group —whether small or large—such as family, friends, colleagues, institutions, society, country, or the world. These various levels of meaning do not exhaust the quest for meaning that the human is engaged in. They could be rewarding or disappointing; in fact, on all these levels, meaningfulness and absurdity are intertwined. That is why these partial meanings may be seen as implicitly or explicitly connected to a general vision (for example: faith in human progress through science, education and technology; a Marxist understanding of society and history; belief in a hereafter; faith in the resurrection,and so on). The overview, or comprehensive meaning, situates and consolidates the partial meanings that we experience at lower levels of meaning.

The comprehensive meaning we learned in our upbringing or at school often remains purely theoretical and does not really speak to us. On the other hand, comprehensive meaning becomes personalized, existential and unifying if it is developed through personal search, enlivened by transcendent experience, and embodied by those who mediate it to us. Searching, in fact, opens people to comprehensive meaning and prepares them to appreciate it, for searching helps them to become aware of their limits and shortcomings in both their pursuit of values and their quest for meaning. The experience of transcendence shows them, in an affective and intuitive manner, something great that is beyond them and attracts them. The presence of mediators—those who have discovered and accepted a comprehensive meaning—makes this comprehensive meaning real and plausible. Mediators show comprehensive meaning lighting the way in the lives and commitments of inspiring and credible individuals.

In the Christian tradition, the great mediator of comprehensive meaning is Jesus Christ. The direction of his earthly life and the choices he made constitute the way and the truth for believers. His love, his freedom, his attention to others, his manner of praying, speaking, acting, suffering and dying, all reveal the comprehensive context in which we can situate our own existence. By raising Jesus, God sanctions his life and teaching and declares them to be more human than any other. Accordingly, an existence modelled on that of Jesus participates in the very meaning that God wishes for every human being.

Although God reveals comprehensive meaning in Jesus, he does not invite the believer to imitate the divine incarnate Son physically or to express their perceptions of meaning in the same way as Jesus of Nazareth. The discovery of a comprehensive meaning takes many forms; it is made in relation to dense human experiences, characterized by the presence of partial meanings and partial non-meanings. Consequently, everyone should be able to express the comprehensive meaning of their life in words that refer to their dense human experiences and to the concrete pursuit of values and meaning accompanying those experiences.

For example, those dedicated to the development and liberation of a certain group of people should be able to identify the dense experiences in which they discovered—positively or negatively—values such as justice, dignity of the person, solidarity, creativity, hope: this or that activity or commitment, this or that project, group, stage of life, social or cultural movement. For the sake of internal coherence, they should also be able to put their comprehensive meaning into dynamic relationship with the lower levels of meaning clarified by those existentially perceived values. Finally, comprehensive meaning normally defines personal identity and allows the person to believe in the value of their contribution to their environment, envisaging it as a contribution to the progress of the reign of God.

The discovery of a comprehensive meaning is not the exclusive privilege of those who call themselves Christians. Sincere searching and transcendent experience lead many people to anticipate a superior quality of life. The quest for meaning and contact with a value that transcends the person brings forth a call to embody that value more (whether we are talking about human love, community, justice, com-

munication, personal balance, or *joie de vivre*). Discovering a comprehensive meaning is a source of hope, for it teaches us over and over
that a meaningful life is possible. Of course we have no formal proof
of it, but we feel invited to enter the game of life, a game that might
be tough and cruel but where the odds of winning are pretty good.
We begin to see that in the end life might not be a tragedy but rather
a comedy in that humour, laughter, and celebration will win out over
sorrow and tears. The discovery of comprehensive meaning reveals
to us a horizon where the brightness of the sun is stronger than the
darkness of the night.

4. Religious conversion

Religious conversion is a free response to a call. This call from God
is expressed by the first three components of the Christian experience,
that is, the search for values and meaning, the experience of transcendence, and the discovery of a comprehensive meaning revealed in Jesus.
Through our decision to believe, we opt for the One who has planted
our search for God within us, as well as our ability to intuit God in the
transcendent, and to recognize God in the incarnate Son.

Faith in God, the Source and Master of existence, corresponds to a
fundamental disposition or basic attitude towards life. This attitude may
be expressed as secular faith in love, in life, or in the great human values.
The motivation for this secular faith is made specific and enriched by
confessional faith, that is to say, by the faith that acknowledges Jesus
as comprehensive meaning, the Father as the one who raised Jesus and
has made human beings co-creators with him, and the Holy Spirit as
the one who liberates us by making us able to receive and give love.
While secular faith, often implicit, relies on the energy and richness
of Life, Christian faith affirms the personal and trinitarian character of
this Life as well as its historic manifestation. The drive and the commitment, however, remain similar, as they include faith in oneself and
in others, which is to say faith in the irreplaceable contribution and
unique calling of every human person. But Christians are fortunate to
be able to graft their faith onto the faith that Jesus had in himself, in
those he met, and in his heavenly Father.

Faith has two inseparable aspects: receiving Someone and following
a message, the presence of a Person and good news. We shall return to

the second aspect when we deal with intellectual conversion, namely, the manner in which we appropriate the meaning of the event of Jesus Christ and its consequences. The important thing to emphasize here is the priority of the first aspect, namely the living relationship with the personal, triune God. Believing is not only being aware of a mysterious Visitor knocking at the door, but also opening the door and letting the Person in, even should the Visitor take up all the room, given the infinite nature of the divine. In the presence of a Guest like this, it is not surprising that we should hesitate, even step back ("Go away from me, Lord, for I am a sinful man!" Luke 5:8). It is a healthy reaction, from a religious point of view, to be astonished at this fantastic relationship that Jesus wants to establish with us.

Faith demands an act of trust, for we feel that God not only connects with us but also transcends us through what he offers us in Jesus. Even though God's plans and our aspirations may coincide, there is also a sense in which God's views and ours are not in agreement. Depending on whether or not we are in harmony with Jesus' values and choices, we will see God's invitations as wisdom one moment and lunacy the next. At certain times, the experience of faith will bring forth in us abundant light and confidence, while at other times, faith will consist of obeying without understanding, listening with intellectual submission to the Word whose deeper meaning escapes us. In accepting a truth that is beyond ourselves, revealed in Jesus and handed down by the church, we experience an openness—which is difficult at the time, but so very rewarding in the long run—to seeing humanity from a divine perspective.

Lastly, the Holy Spirit produces in us the conviction and the decision to believe. This conviction grows thanks to our experience of human values, love, meaning, and absurdity. It springs forth from our observation of a complicity between our deep desires and the word of God. This conviction is not rooted in apologetic argumentation, but rather in our hearts, where God's love is poured forth. This conviction is, however, never so absolute as to interfere with our freedom to accept or reject the Gospel.

5. Psychological and moral conversion

While religious conversion consists of turning towards God and accepting the relationship that God wishes to establish with us, psychological and moral conversion consists of "evangelizing" our horizontal relationships. The dynamic of religious experience is such that religious conversion influences psychological and moral conversion: "Beloved, since God loved us so much, we also ought to love one another" (1 John 4:11). Our faith can thus have a decisive impact on our ethics, on the orientation of our actions. Our faith invites us to situate our pursuit of values in a particular context, namely that of the reign of God in the process of being realized. Knowing that God is the source and goal of these human values, that Jesus gave his life for us, and that we here on earth are preparing the coming of a new world, underscores the gravity and urgency of moral commitment.

Psychological and moral conversion transforms our fundamental attitude to life. The ultimate purpose of existence is no longer a guilt-assuaging conformism or the pursuit of pleasure or well-being; neither is it an individualistic actualization of self, or a masochistic or fanatical giving of self. Instead, the believers' main concern is to make a loving contribution to the realization of the Creator's plan for humanity. God's will becomes the ultimate criterion for their behaviour. But, for their actions to be appropriate and effective, they will need to be attentive to what truly benefits others. They will need to fine-tune their ethical judgment and develop emotional balance.

Being faithful to the demands of both the Gospel and psychological authenticity brings believers face to face with the paradox of self-realization. They know that self-realization is not achieved by putting one's own pleasure before that of others, for such selfishness results only in bitter satisfaction; nor is it achieved by doing the opposite—ensuring the pleasure of others at the expense of one's own—for altruism of this type, founded on self-denial, engenders resentment and hostility. How do believers get around this dilemma? In fact, it is neither a matter of self-centredness nor one of self-denial. It is, rather, a question of turning towards that reality which calls out for our involvement, the promotion of true human good, of choosing the kind of action that suits who we are. What can we do to come out of our shells and develop our potential? We can be open to new interests, respond to values that call out to us, give our active support to a project, a "cause," a goal that focuses our energies and gives meaning to our life. Beyond egocentrism and altruism, the Christian ethic is one of doing good by participating in the building of the Kingdom of God.

This experience of fruitfulness and generativity involves both suffering and joy. "When a woman is in labour, she has pain, because her hour has come. But when her child is born, she no longer remembers her anguish because of the joy of having brought a human being into the world" (John 16:21). Psychological and moral conversion consists in finding one's joy in giving birth to and fostering the growth of persons, including oneself. From this perspective we should interpret Jesus' saying, "Those who lose their life for my sake, and for the sake of the gospel, will save it" (Mark 8:35), and the law of the cross, which is just as much the law of existence as the law of the Gospel. Following in Jesus' footsteps, we save our life—that is, our personality at its deepest level—by placing it at the service of others. If we are concerned with ourselves, it should be to welcome that life that God wants to give us abundantly, as well as to become more capable of loving, for there is no greater joy than to love while knowing that our love is not in vain. What is more, this joy becomes deeper the better we understand that the work we are involved in is not primarily a human undertaking: rather, it is the Holy Spirit who animates and guarantees its success. This work, the building up of the body of Christ (Eph. 4:16), can draw us out of our individualistic cocoons and help us situate our self-realization in a collective context. Every member or part of the human body in fact acts in terms of the whole, according to a mysterious organic law called mutual assistance or interdependence. Therefore, if humanity forms one body and if the Holy Spirit guarantees its growth and final perfection, our concern for self-realization may be integrated into a broader horizon and deeper motivation.

Finally, psychological and moral conversion intensifies our sense of sin. Sin is not the guilt associated with the transgression of a law, but an omission or failure (rejecting an appropriate good, that is, a desirable life-giving possibility in a concrete situation) in relation to God's plan for humanity. Sin is thus a human reality—the absence of love, a failure to bring forth good fruit—but experienced in relation to the reign of God. To sin is to go against what God desires for a particular person or group. This is why faith enables the Christian to perceive more clearly the seriousness of sin, while situating it in the context of forgiveness and salvation.

6. Intellectual conversion

To convert one's intelligence or "evangelize" one's mind is to acquire a Christian interpretation of life: a vision of existence that is ordered and consistent within itself, faithful to the word of God and spirit of Jesus, and open to the culture of one's time. This long-term undertaking is of prime importance in a world where a love of God and of neighbour that is not accompanied by intellectual discernment would necessarily be subject to manipulation and could end up serving interests that are in fact contrary to the genuine promotion of human good.

The first condition of intellectual conversion is to have an open mind towards the Gospel with a view to appropriating the revealed message. This consists of finding out what, in Christian belief, speaks the most to the individual or group concerned, given the orientation of their searching, their transcendent experiences and the way they understand the comprehensive meaning manifested in Jesus. The tradition of faith and the teaching of the church are received by trying to express them in one's own words, in a kind of personal or communal credo that coincides with the journey actually being travelled. This assumes there will be ongoing development of interpretation, as well as a concern for ordering and prioritizing in the world of one's convictions and ideas—distinguishing between the essential and the secondary, the permanent and the variable, and identifying points of emphasis and importance without making them absolutes.

Second, this intellectual process requires frequent realignment with Jesus. The believer looks at Jesus in order to discover how he looks at others: at people, society, life, and the world. Jesus looks with the eyes of one who has let himself be permeated by the Creator's love. Likewise, anyone who lets God love her and who interiorizes the hope for God's reign cannot help but see with new eyes all that goes on around them. In practice, what this means is that her stance is both receptive and critical towards the mentalities she encounters, which contribute to shaping her vision of life.

The third requirement for intellectual conversion concerns precisely this attitude made up of both receptivity and a critical mindset towards the opinions, principles of conduct and ideologies that abound in our society. It would be an illusion to think that our faith is not influenced by the beliefs conveyed by the culture around us: our faith is always subject to inculturation. The important thing is to ensure that this inculturation process takes place with as much awareness as possible. It is good for believers to be open-minded towards anthropological models, images or ideals regarding the human person, moral doctrines, and so forth. These notions contain resources and potential that we may use in our effort to understand ourselves as human beings and achieve self-realization. In other respects, Christians need to be forcefully critical of certain of their contemporaries' modes of thinking. This work is made all the more difficult by the fact that very often these modes of thinking have been internalized: they have become our own. Nevertheless, the word of God invites us to make this effort of intellectual purification, since our action and our service in the world are directly influenced by these opinions and convictions. "Do not be conformed to this world, but be transformed by the renewing of your minds, so that you may discern what is the will of God—what is good and acceptable and perfect" (Romans 12:2).

7. Prayer

Prayer impregnates all the other components of Christian experience, but it especially enables one to live out the fourth component, direct relationship with God. Prayer is just that: the relationship with God fully assumed, that is, consciously and freely enhanced to the point of dialogue. It is characterized by a movement from an Unknown to a "You": whereas we wondered about the mystery, felt attracted by it, reflected on and perhaps discussed it, we henceforth speak to God and listen to him. Prayer, however, remains difficult to define, for it has contrasting elements: activity and passivity, attentiveness and surrender, offering and welcome, speaking and silence, moral exigency and gratuitousness, and so forth.

To pray is to be present to a Presence, to be directly present to an incomparable Presence. While it is true that God reaches us through the mediation of phenomena outside us—events, what we read, works of art, spoken words, individuals and groups—God reaches us more directly through our inner life. We know our inner life to the extent that we have become capable of being present to ourselves. Through our feelings and our questions, as well as our experience of understanding, pursuing values, choosing and loving, we sense within ourselves a desire to know and to be loved, and a capacity to love and to act, which together constitute our living consciousness. To pray is to place ourselves in the presence of the One who is the source of this consciousness and who alone can fill it.

Jesus' example stimulates us to cultivate this relationship with the Creator which, from our very depths, engenders existence and life. His moral commitment likewise invites us to avoid the trap of a regressive immediacy which, by virtue of its immature search for security, for fusion and for warmth, would be like a return to the mother's breast. On the contrary, our immediacy with the God of Jesus is adult and responsible to the extent that we associate ourselves with the struggle of God's Son in today's world. True Christian prayer helps us to pay increasing attention to human reality and to actively discern there the reign of God making its way with our help. Indeed, faith in Jesus impels us to praise a God whose concern, throughout history and in the present, has been the human good. It moves us to demand that we live in dynamic harmony with the realization of God's loving plan.

Our conscious relationship with God in prayer is naturally expressed through symbol. Symbolism links the body, the imagination, and the emotions with inner prayer. Realized in myriad forms of artistic expression—for example, architecture, decor, body movement, song, poetry—the symbolic and sacramental mode makes the historical presence of God in Jesus real and visible through rituals that bring it to mind. Liturgy enables us to embody our relationship with God in our whole being and thus allows us to integrate all the dimensions of our faith. This is the power—internalizing as well as externalizing—of the symbol.

8. Ecclesial kinship

"It is not good that the man should be alone" (Genesis 2:18). From the time of infancy, every individual develops in relationship with others. In the family, in the group or in the couple, the "I" unites with others and constitutes with them a "we" which takes on an instinct of solidarity. The relational character of the human is what makes us capable of sharing, supporting, assisting. It is what prompts us to give and receive, to offer and to welcome. Humans are social animals in that they function solely with reference to other presences, whether these are physically visible or not. Therefore, the experience of the Gospel, which assumes the whole of the human being, necessarily includes a dimension of intersubjective kinship, which we call ecclesial kinship.

This ecclesial kinship can be experienced on two levels. On the first level, we note that God reaches us by acting through others. When we reflect on the key experiences of our life, we can observe that a great many people have helped us become who we are, while others may have hurt us. If, through these contacts, we have known trust and solidarity, and if we have learned how to use our sufferings and our failures, we have no doubt discovered that our neighbour is not primarily a threat, but a human being like ourselves who, often unwittingly, enables us to meet ourselves and to meet Jesus. It is in this way that our sister or brother becomes for us the sacrament or sign of God. We understand then that God loves us through others and that he loves others through us; we discern Christ in ourselves and in those we meet.

The second level of ecclesial kinship is the experience of community. This becomes possible when we enter into contact with a Christian community and discover its strength. The community, in fact, is a place where each of us may be welcomed and recognized, where we share our perceptions of the meaning of life, where we celebrate our faith, and where we give one another mutual support in the service of others. We experience church first and foremost in a local community and there we learn quite naturally to be open to the diocesan and universal church. Having sought and partially found communion on a smaller scale, even with the inevitable problems and tensions inherent in any gathering, it is normal that we should also desire to see it on regional, national and international levels, and that we should make Jesus' project our own: Jesus came into the world "to gather into one the dispersed children of God" (John 11:52). In this context, the institutional church stands at the service of this divine design, as guardian of God's word and place of messianic hope.

9. Service

This component of our Gospel experience stems from our existence in the world, that is, the fact that we are physical bodies located within nature. Human beings have physical needs that must be satisfied: food, clothing, accommodation, etc. They also have fundamental psychological needs: sexuality, family, education, leisure, and so forth. According to Matthew's gospel, we will be judged on our response to these basic needs: did we provide food and drink, did we clothe and look after strangers, the sick and prisoners (Matt. 25:35-36)?

The long cultural, scientific, and technical evolution of humanity represents an immense effort to satisfy physical and psychological needs. However, today, just as in the past, service is carried out primarily in the form of work. Work will always require effort, but it is important that we reduce the burden of work as much as possible by using technology and psychology judiciously. What we must improve are not only the physical conditions of work but, more particularly, the climate around interpersonal relations at work and the way they are organized. A great effort of the imagination will be required if we wish to see the standing of the worker improved. In family life, industry, business, health care, education, and the other sectors of public life, aspirations for dignity, democratization, competence, and justice represent a huge challenge.

If Christians want to engage in the kind of human activity that translates into service, they cannot afford to be conformists or slackers. We are talking about salvation of the whole person, which is not just about one's relationship with God, but which is incarnated in everything that contributes to humanizing and liberating life. Certainly, salvation takes for granted religious conversion, where we accept God's love, and psychological and moral conversion, where we develop fundamental attitudes that enable us to love our neighbour as ourselves. But these attitudes must animate our behaviour and transform structures. In a world of aberrant behaviours and unjust structures, the experience of the reign of God as in the process of realization is only authentic when we become aware that the reign of God itself reaches out to change alienating situations. The evangelical spirit must be strong enough to set off interactions of liberation aimed at changing dehumanizing socio-economic relationships. When this concern for effectiveness goes hand in hand with a truly Christian vision and motivation, salvation comes to the whole human person, both physically and spiritually.

Service is one of two aspects of Christian mission in the world. God gave humankind the responsibility of developing the world: "Be fruitful and multiply, and fill the earth and subdue it; and have dominion over the fish of the sea and over the birds of the air and over every living thing that moves upon the earth" (Genesis 1:28). Through the prophets, God reminds us of the concern that the earth's resources be shared by all. Through Jesus, God teaches us how to carry out that first exhortation by serving our sisters and brothers: "So, if I, your Lord and Teacher, have washed your feet, you also ought to wash one another's feet. For I have set you an example, that you also should do as I have done to you" (John 13:14-15). This first aspect of mission is complemented by a second, namely, communication, through which people tell one another the meaning of their service and of their earthly life.

10. Communication

Communication is realized in three ways: dialogue, witness and evangelization.

Dialogue is a form of communication that takes place in an atmosphere of free exchange. Through verbal and non-verbal language alike, both parties are enriched in human experience and bring together their quests for meaning and wisdom. We introduce the other to our world and are welcomed into hers or his. We experience in turn openness, confusion, sharing of convictions, questioning, confrontation, diverging views, and so forth. This sharing of feelings and intuitions, this exchange of ideas and viewpoints, is indispensable if we wish to broaden our horizons by encountering in their uniqueness a variety of people and trends. The Roman playwright Terence said, "As I am human, nothing human is foreign to me." Dialogue involves an irreplaceable experience of reciprocity which the evangelizer as such cannot afford, at least most of the time, for the evangelizer needs to focus on the needs, questions and problems of others who approach him or her as a representative of the church. It is therefore important that the person exercising evangelical responsibility also be capable, outside of work, of openness to opportunities for dialogue where he or she may be challenged and may listen to others without having to direct them towards living the Gospel.

Another form of communication is witness. Jesus asked the first disciples to be witnesses to his resurrection: "You will be my witnesses in Jerusalem, in all Judea and Samaria, and to the ends of the earth" (Acts 1:8). In our pluralist society with its secular institutions, Christians will be witnesses of Jesus first of all by the quality of their service, since people are touched especially by actions. However, action is not enough: the action must be motivated by the Gospel and reflect Gospel attitudes. What speaks to people is not just the fact of being served, but being served by someone who has been or is in the process of being converted. Moreover, giving witness is not always done alone: gatherings of the local Christian community or of the wider Christian community, as well as the numerous vehicles of collective Christian commitment, can speak very eloquently to our contemporaries.

When people enter into contact and dialogue with active Christians who are attentive to others, they often like to ask them about what motivates them. That is when evangelization in the strict sense becomes possible. Then one can witness in the words of Jesus, our source of meaning and hope. "Always be ready to make your defense to anyone who demands from you an accounting for the hope that is in you" (1 Peter 3:15). While it is good to be able to express your own deep experience, it is also important to bring others to focus on their own experience, in order to accompany them on their quest for meaning and happiness. Meeting a witness of Jesus does not in fact prove decisive unless it helps people to know themselves better, develop as human beings, discover their identity and calling, and approach in a personal way the various components of Christian experience.

Part II

RELATIONSHIP WITH GOD

3

The Act of Christian Faith

We live in an era where many Catholics, unprepared for the need to adapt, have not yet digested the social, cultural and ecclesial changes of the twentieth century and therefore feel great confusion, even deep bewilderment, in the face of the fact that their religious and moral identity has been badly shaken. Moreover, large sectors of the population who consider themselves to be Christian have distanced themselves from the way church authorities define beliefs and standards of behaviour. On the one hand, there is a tendency to repress questions and doubts, to exclude current reinterpretations, to re-affirm dogma rigidly, to restore lost doctrinal unanimity.[1] On the other hand, the motto "To each his own," often associated with bourgeois individualism, is accepted in practice, so long as one sticks to ideas that have meaning for the individual and that help him live his life. We are witnessing a polarization between a doctrinal religion, not adapted to the culture, and a utilitarian religion, retaining from its Christian heritage only that which suits its purpose.

Critical rationality

Refusing to be trapped in this dilemma, I want to be part of a third group, which takes up the challenge of critical adaptation. To adapt in a critical manner involves adapting to one's culture, not passively or slavishly, but distinguishing between those aspects of the culture that are authentic and edifying and those that are artificial and alienating. This concern for measured adaptation takes note of a fact that has indelibly marked the western mind: the so-called Age of Enlightenment. The Enlightenment triumphed in the eighteenth century, was partially neutralized by Romanticism in the nineteenth century, but did not cease to have a deep influence on Europe, the Americas, and even Asia and Africa by way of ideologies linked to science and education.

Rejection and opposition by the church hierarchy and clergy did not prevent a great number of ideas, sometimes good ones, sometimes harmful ones, from gaining currency via movements like scientific rationalism, the desire for democracy, Marxism, psychoanalysis, psychological humanism, the arts and literature, history, sociology. Behind all of these currents, there is a force, critical rationality, which may be just as easily exercised in favour of religion as against it. When Christians see the value of this force, which has become one of the driving forces of their culture, two fundamental attitudes emerge: the search for meaning, and critical questioning. The first attitude, which flourished in the Middle Ages, is traditional: it is called "understanding the faith." The second attitude has not yet received its credentials in the Catholic Church, although many believers adopt it, albeit somewhat uncomfortably. That is why I would like to point out briefly the contribution it makes.

In colleges and universities, on television and at the movies, in books and conversations, thousands of ideas are circulating that represent stumbling blocks to the faith. Even within the church, courses in theology, history, exegesis or catechesis cause many things to be called into question. This situation can either provoke an attitude of entrenchment or serve as a test of growth, purification, and maturing. The problem is much broader than that of "understanding the faith," even if the latter does contribute to the solution. In fact, we need not just understand our faith, but learn intellectual judgment as well. This is why we need to speak of critical rationality. The Greek word *krinein* means to be in crisis, to criticize, to judge. For Christians, to judge means to be engaged in a "negative" task which complements the "positive" understanding one acquires of one's faith. This negative task is carried out when it is necessary to reject ways of seeing that may be very widespread in the church; to deny the major importance that a particular doctrine may hold for many people; to repudiate an intellectual horizon that has become too narrow; to assume the hermeneutic of suspicion practised by Marx, Nietzsche, Freud and extended by feminist or anti-racist thinkers, or by liberation theologians, applied to ideas or behaviours found in Christianity.

Given the news media and today's pluralistic world, Christians must accept the tall order of becoming independent judges, going beyond both sectarian narrowness and facile relativism, making an effort at true dialogue, and consulting sources of meaning and truth. Quite often as a result, a certain naïveté we may have had regarding what we learned as children begins to fall away. It might feel as if we are losing our faith when, in reality, we are being invited to move from the faith of a child to the faith of an adult. The person who is able to judge with wisdom reinterprets their beliefs while at the same time retaining their child-like capacity to admire, dream, trust, and believe in someone. Passing through a period of doubt allows us to shed our first naïveté and move into what philosopher Paul Ricoeur calls second naïveté.[2] We learn to integrate the refreshing attitude of the child and the critical mind of the adult.

Meaning and truth

The solution to this set of problems concerning faith depends on the ability to distinguish between meaning and truth. We are very much attuned to meaning but not very attentive to truth: we spontaneously accept that which is meaningful for us and tell ourselves it must therefore be true. However, the history of science is strewn with hypotheses which made sense, but which facts were unable to confirm. While we accept this requirement of objectivity in science, we might think, wrongly, that subjectivity should prevail in the arts and religion. We do not see that true artists and the great religious minds are quite objective in what they observe and express. We forget that there are criteria for determining whether a work of art or a religious message is authentic or not. Today, many thinkers claim that religious language is purely symbolic and they exclude the possibility that there can be clear doctrines. We shall see in Chapter 12, for example, how on the one hand, Dürckheim dismisses the possibility of being able to determine, with the help of technical vocabulary, whether a transcendent reality exists, while, on the other hand, he himself cannot help but interpret this reality in a very precise manner. Similarly, Rousseau's position towards the world's great religions states that they are all valid, although, for pragmatic reasons only, it is preferable to stay with the one in which we were raised.

Thus, the subjectivist attitude that our contemporaries adopt so naturally on religious matters presents a major problem for Catholicism.

Catholicism, indeed, continues to hold its deep conviction that the Christian faith includes, concurrently with an interpersonal relationship with God, an affirmative response to the revelation of specific truths regarding the Trinity, creation and humankind, as well as certain salvific events that have actually taken place. Now, the distinction between meaning and truth allows for great freedom of interpretation within the faith. Loyalty to revelation requires that we accept the whole of what the church holds to be true. But, once this general adhesion to the essential statement of the Creed is granted, there is room for an entire development of personal or community appropriation of the meaning of what is revealed. For 2000 years, Christians' efforts to interpret their beliefs have produced an enormous variety of viewpoints. One would have to be quite unaware of the history of the church to be scandalized by the current pluralism: it is not a new phenomenon.

For believers, the search for meaning precedes, accompanies, and extends an act of faith that includes adhesion to established beliefs. Unfortunately, Catholicism's idea of doctrine is often seen as blind obedience, accepted by some and rejected by others. It is regrettable that so many people consider Christian obedience to religious truth as something unusual, either as necessary or as indefensible. Actually, this response of faith to a revealed truth is not isolated from the rest of life. To prove this, it needs to be shown that humans, insofar as they are mentally and morally healthy, fundamentally seek to know reality, whether in the world of action, or in science, art or religion.

Openness to reality

Freud proposed a most useful distinction between the pleasure principle, focused on the immediate, and the reality principle, which looks to long-term results. This distinction shows it is possible for the human animal to look past the tip of their nose. Unfortunately, Freud limits reality to the material and biological aspect of the world. The positivist philosophy of the end of the nineteenth century, which he never moved beyond, did not allow him to see the whole impact of human intentionality. The human spirit, in fact, displays a spontaneous intention, albeit sometimes at a great cost, to respect five levels of reality.[3]

On the first level, we receive the data from the senses, the imagination and memory. Everything we see, hear, perceive (through the senses or through sophisticated techniques), everything we investigate, everything we learn in our conversations or readings may be useful and, depending on the matter at issue, is worth recording or taking into account. We feel we cannot dismiss the experience, that we must pay attention to the data. On the second level, we ask questions that lead to understanding the data. Our questioning manifests a desire to find a meaning in phenomena or behaviours that intrigue us. A light goes on when we grasp the reason or the explanation. But once this intellectual grasp has been articulated, we may ask ourselves whether it is true. That is when we move to the third level. We experience the need to verify whether the idea or hypothesis we have formed corresponds to reality. We appeal to relatively complex verification criteria and try to ascertain what degree of probability or certitude we have reached. The fourth level is that of values, decisions and action. In intentional feelings which, contrary to purely basic feelings, reveal deep realities, we see the attraction and beauty of things, living beings and persons. We are then able to ask ourselves about what is worth being and doing. In a world of numerous but limited possibilities, in the face of unequal or incompatible goods, we ask ourselves what is best in a given situation. Then we must follow our conscience while at the same time informing it; in order to evaluate well, we must be inspired by love and pay attention to the pertinent data so as to grasp its relevance for the matter in question. Furthermore, the moral quality of individuals is determined not only by their practical understanding, but also by the congruency between their value judgments and their actions. Finally, the fifth level is that of religion, which manifests itself in two ways. There are transcendent experiences through which we feel emotionally that we are open to an infinite reality that attracts us. Then there are the fundamental questions that human beings ask themselves concerning meaning, truth, values and love, which show we are open to something more than the first four levels can offer. Simply contemplating finite reality does not enable us to answer questions of the kind that Gauguin inscribed on his large Polynesian painting: "Where do we come from? What are we? Where are we going?" While they are difficult and mysterious, these questions of religious import are to be taken seriously because they are reasonable and universal.

Anyone engaged in a process of self-knowledge can consult these five levels of their lived experience. They will observe that their intellect, when it is functioning soundly, seeks to know reality on all its levels. On the other hand, if they are honest, they will also admit that they can easily make a mistake. In the religious realm in particular, if one proceeds solely on one's own strength, one will wind up with a mixture of truth and error. Now, this problem of error must be seen in relation to an amazing affirmation which one notes so often in the Bible, namely that the vision of reality that is expressed there comes from God. In the Judeo-Christian tradition, the ultimate criterion for religious truth does not reside in the human intellect, but in this divine revelation. This revelation is mediated by the prophets' and the biblical writers' intelligence, and by the reflection underlying the doctrinal declarations of the church. In order that religious truth, so difficult to ascertain and affirm with confidence, may be accessible to many, the Holy Spirit guarantees that the church sets out a correct overall interpretation, whatever limitation might affect the perspectives and particular teaching of the pope and the bishops. As long as we do not submit naïvely to every single word spoken by the church hierarchy, access to divine revelation is truly liberating, for it connects us with the deepest reality there is.

The levels in the act of faith

Let us look now at the various intellectual and affective operations that make up the act of Christian faith. I have organized these components according to the structure of intentionality. They are, however, not presented in chronological order. They complement one another, act upon one another and make the act of faith a deep and complex adventure inspired by the Holy Spirit.

On the first level of the human spirit, the Hebrew Scriptures and the Christian tradition together offer a body of data: stories, beliefs, images and metaphors, liturgical practices, and live witness. The writings, the people and the events are intermediaries likely to pique our curiosity and rouse our interest.

On the second level, this data can provide occasions for questioning. In the Bible and in Christian believers, we may observe a hope that relies on affirmations concerning the meaning of life. The great questions regarding existence have been asked throughout Judeo-Christian history. Since this history produces as many questions as answers, it is important to determine what questions the affirmations of faith are answering. These questions are easier to discern with respect to the existence of God, for example, than with respect to salvation and the divine sonship of Jesus. This is why, in Chapter 6, I shall try to present what the resurrection allowed the disciples to understand about Jesus. Thus, the light shed by the Bible, religious teaching, liturgy, and Christian witnesses who help and stimulate us, not only gives life meaning but also invites us to ask questions about truth.

On the third level of intentionality, human beings wonder about the truth of the meaning they have found. It requires well-developed and bold intellectual honesty to admit that there are objectively true religious answers. Where can one find these answers, if not in the religious traditions? Now, among these traditions, the Catholic Church claims with singular insistence that it is able to offer answers that are true. At this stage, the person sincere in their search takes seriously the extraordinary declaration of this church, according to which: the Holy Spirit spoke through the prophets and to the biblical writers; God the Son became human and revealed who the Father is; the church is guided by the Holy Spirit, who thus makes it an infallible witness to the truth. Even if this truth is expressed in various ways according to different cultures and may be formulated differently in dialogue with the non-Christian religions, its essential core has been the same for 2000 years. When making a reality judgment that will have far-reaching consequences, one considers as real the fact that God has revealed himself, one welcomes the Christian message as the word of God, and one adheres to the truth taught by the church. We need to remember, however, that the distinction between truth and meaning allows for a freedom of interpretation within a specific culture. On the one hand, we need to accept the truth with the overall meaning which tradition has given it; on the other, the appropriation of this tradition in an evolving culture demands a certain creativity with respect to interpretation. There are numerous grounds of credibility able to lead us to the reality judgment that characterizes the third level. But the intellectual act whereby one adheres to Christianity goes beyond grounds of credibility, for it relies on the word of God, the only reliable and sure foundation in the religious realm.

Let us move now to the fourth level. The question posed here is, "Is believing a good thing?" In the case of an affirmative answer, one moves on to the value judgment which considers that one must believe, then to the decision to make an act of faith, and finally, to conduct whereby one tries to put into practice the Good News one has received. The grounds of credibility that motivate making this value judgment are many. First of all, there is everything that belongs to the second level: the more one finds meaning in the Christian experience, the more one is inclined to believe. Next, one is anxious to make certain that the Bible (in its central message), the character of Jesus, the witness given by the first disciples, and the church's claims regarding its transmission of truth, do not contradict reason and human values. The interest, admiration and attraction felt towards Jesus also play a part: the kind of man he was, the way he lived, his message, his choices, his attitudes and his actions, his practical and existential response to the problem of evil, sin, and liberation.

The deep dynamic of faith, however, comes from a love that is far stronger than all of these considerations—although they contribute to nourishing it—and which belongs to the fifth level of intentional experience. On this final level, we find the affective motivation for believing. This motivation is rooted in the Christian experience of transcendence, in which one discovers God in Jesus. In this experience we discern the overwhelming love of the Father at work in the life, passion, death, and resurrection of Jesus. We see for ourselves the action of the Holy Spirit, who lets us glimpse the infinite love of God in the goodness, friendship and forgiveness of Jesus. At this interpersonal level a living relationship is established between believers and God. This aspect of faith consists of a religious conversion, in which we welcome God's presence with gratitude and agree to live by this transcendent love. The transformation of the essence of human intentionality is a gift of the Holy Spirit, who plants the very love of God in the hearts of believers.

As we can see, the act of Christian faith is made up of a series of discoveries, never completed, always to be pursued and deepened. Faith is a complex reality, even in simple people. It cannot be reduced to an arbitrary and extrinsic gift from God, nor to a mere assent of the mind, through which one would be granted salvation; nor to blind submission without any rational critique, nor to simple trust without affirmation concerning reality. It is neither a quest for meaning limited to a philosophy of life, nor an absolutely ineffable spiritual experience which no council or theology would be able to describe. In positive terms, one must say that Christian faith is an action of the Holy Spirit that transcends but also includes human operations involving the intellect, the emotions, and the will. It is an encounter with God which goes beyond language but which, through the use of precise language, may be situated in relation to the rest of human experience and all that is real.

4

Ideologies and Disillusionment

Following the Second World War, North Americans experienced thirty years of economic prosperity and material abundance. During this period, they discovered that many changes were possible in the way society is organized and functions. They expressed their dreams and they tried to realize them in industry, business, the public service, unions, education, health care, human rights, and various institutions for social welfare. However, during the seventies, people became disappointed and disillusioned by the results of these great efforts of social transformation. The causes of this after-effect are the domain of economics and social psychology, and not for me to present here. I am more interested in another type of cause, namely, the ideologies that allowed those particular dreams to be realized and strategies for change to be developed. One may identify four great ideologies which, in tension with one another, all contributed to shaping the mentalities of the 1945–1975 period: social-democratic liberalism, Marxism, the "spiritual psychology" movement and, in the Christian context, a progressive vision of the Kingdom of God.

The purpose of this chapter is to describe these ideologies and show their inadequacy with regard to hope. I would remind you, at the outset, that a theological critique of contemporary ideologies has nothing to gain by denigrating the individuals who believe in them. Each of these ideologies is a vehicle for dreams and includes blueprints for action that are a credit to humanity. What we are trying to do here, rather, is bring to light the deficiencies in their understanding of human life and life in society, for in the end it is these deficiencies that disappoint the hope placed in these ideologies.

Social-democratic liberalism

It is almost a contradiction in terms to speak of social-democratic liberalism. Yet, in the period following the war, which raised so much hope, the dominant ideology in the West was characterized by the combination of capitalist free enterprise and the initiative of the State. We must not underestimate the impact of this odd alliance of, on the one hand, forces of production and business which, when all was said and done, were structured in a fairly standard manner, and on the other, socialist programs aiming to give a great number of people access to material well-being. This type of compromise between divergent, but not irreconcilable, interests represents a pragmatism that, in contrast to oligarchical interventions, has the merit of not stifling creativity.

Nevertheless, creativity can go in directions that are not always beneficial and can be hijacked by groups that think only of increasing and protecting their own advantage. For instance, what begins as perfectly valid unionism turns into a corporatism that focuses on privileges for the worker elite. Or, the rules of the financial game—which are supposed to stimulate the economy—end up, through huge territorial, energy, or tax concessions, bringing disproportionate gain to plutocratic minorities at the expense of the majority of the people, both inside first-world countries and between first- and third- or fourth-world countries. As long as Westerners held on to the illusion that they could simultaneously continue increasing their wealth and gradually eliminate poverty, the ideology of a liberalism open to social democracy was firmly maintained. It was the era when principles like "education brings advancement" did not yet appear ridiculous. The problems of poor countries were attributed to the fact that they were "underdeveloped," and so, with the help of the great industrialized nations, they could become "developing" countries.

What form of hope did this ideology inspire? It was a form of optimism nourished by prosperity and abundance, unaware that it was following incompatible goals and would have to make fundamental choices sooner or later. In view of this, it is not surprising that, as a result of reflections on Chinese and Cuban Marxism, student protests denounced the contradictions of the pragmatically established system and vigorously proposed a new way of thinking.

Marxism

Despite its influence among intellectuals, Marxism has not achieved a single conquest in the West in fifty years. In North America, no communist party grew to the point of being able to play an important role. In Europe, most people saw thinkers like Karl Popper and Raymond Aron as the winners in the debates with the Marxists. The abrupt end to the "Prague Spring," Solzhenitsyn's revelations concerning the Gulags, and China's progressive about-face in the aftermath of its Cultural Revolution are all factors that entered into Marxism's being discredited.

It is important to do more here than simply record—with regret for some and consolation for others—the fading of Marxist ideology in the contemporary world. What must be emphasized is the similarity that exists between Marxism and liberalism despite their differences. With respect to a Christian vision of hope, in fact, these two ideologies are forms of optimism. As they both belong to the evolutionism of the eighteenth and nineteenth centuries, they presuppose that human nature is capable of progress on all levels, and are unable to offer any kind of hope that would be consonant with the tragic character of human existence.

For its part, liberalism holds as certain the idea that simply applying individual initiative in the economic sphere produces without fail, at least in the long term, collective wealth. Have we ever been credulous, these two hundred years, to accept the secular notion of Providence expressed by Adam Smith in his image of the invisible hand so admirably regulating the market of trade and distribution! There is no more eloquent testimony to the human tendency to justify the hopes of their class with a general theory. In this particular case, the theory relies on an arbitrary faith and represents an insult to the majority of the world who live in poverty.

In Marxism, on the other hand, the general theory of how to envisage humanity's historical journey appears more dramatic than that of liberalism. It opens our eyes to the misery of the many and defines some of its causes. It does not subscribe to the hypothesis of social and economic harmony that the mechanisms of free enterprise are considered to favour automatically. It advocates a reversal in the way ownership and the exchange of goods are structured, to be achieved through revolutionary political action. But once the revolution has been won, the manner of organizing collective life relapses into one that strangely resembles that of non-communist countries. The same confidence in technology and the same vision of a "one-dimensional human being" govern its social analysis. Problems to do with organization, competence, creativity, and morality appear once again, curiously similar to those which historians and experts in the human sciences note in other political systems and in other cultures. Confronted by such paradoxes, the fundamental inadequacy of post-revolutionary Marxism's optimism became apparent.

The "spiritual psychology" movement

Since the seventies, a psychology movement with a spiritual leaning has enjoyed a certain popularity. Without replacing the two major social ideologies, it has succeeded in complementing them by providing, outside the disappointing realms of work and social and political institutions, a type of hope that focuses on the individual. By the "spiritual psychology" movement, I mean the philosophy of life that accompanies counselling practices, personal growth sessions and therapy sessions. What is in question here is not the value of the therapists or the validity of their methods, but rather the vision of the human being that accompanies them. Now, in this so-called humanist branch of North American psychology, or the branch Maslow called the third force (alongside the Freudian school and the experiential-positivist-behavioural stream), we find a view of human nature that is the exact opposite of Protestant pessimism: it emphasizes, in a rhetorical fashion, the potential of the person seeking self-actualization.

This optimism provoked a reaction: for about twenty-five years now, certain popular authors have been attacking this psychological movement, labelling it a narcissistic cult of the self that evades social realities. Alongside these extremist opponents, balanced critics have pointed out the frequently anti-intellectual nature of psychological practices. They consider that these practices focus on the emotional aspect of direct interpersonal relations and ignore an analysis of the structural and situational content that serves as the basis for the reality judgments and value judgments that guide our actions. By emphasizing this affective side, psychological practices confine themselves to small-group processes and reinforce the traditional dichotomy between private and public domains. Moreover, while most psychologists reject—and rightly so—legalistic moralities, they have not succeeded in developing a dynamic morality that is up to the standard of their professional competence. As it is only natural for them to be seeking wisdom and ethical directions, they venture into the sphere of moral philosophy as amateurs easily drawn into facile solutions, paradoxes and even contradictions (I am thinking here of authors like Maslow, Fromm, and Lowen).

In connection with the "spiritual psychology" movement discussed above, I wish to acknowledge the openness to the spiritual by many psychologists (for example, R.D. Laing, Frankl, Maslow, Fromm). We must be grateful to them without, however, ignoring the ambiguity of this openness. The spiritual aspect here proves most of the time to be more an extension of human self rather than a confrontation with a personal Reality. The great religions are often robbed of their substance and exploited by the "spiritual psychology" movement as vague sources of inspiration towards egocentric growth. Harvey Cox insists that the bits of Eastern religion transposed into the West are thereby significantly re-interpreted, even distorted, simply by virtue of being inserted into the cultural context of the individualistic affirmation of the self.[4]

Like social-democratic liberalism, the "spiritual psychology" movement constitutes a questionable mixture, and is also a vehicle for superficial hope. However, people have only recently begun to be disappointed by its optimism.

A progressive vision of the Kingdom of God

The last form of ideology I would like to examine briefly is the progressive vision of the Kingdom of God, which has come to dominate many Christian circles in the last thirty-five years. It is found in two distinct versions. The first version, already presented in the works of Teilhard de Chardin and forcefully articulated at the time of the Second Vatican Council, consists of a manner of understanding the Kingdom of God that is similar to the evolutionism of liberal societies. It looks to earthly realities and discerns in movements like global communication, socialism, or feminism signs of the times that make the Kingdom visible. The second version is closer to Marxism, particularly the Marxism of Ernst Bloch, who influenced German political theology and Latin American liberation theology. Two stages of the Kingdom—the absolute future and the temporal future—in this world are confused. The future is understood as an immense reservoir of possibilities understood in terms of earthly practices and structures. By virtue of the new, not only is the status quo rejected, but also a this-worldly ethic that is based on past experience and bears the stamp of realism. The reign of God permits a daring that dismisses the possibilities measured by history, the human sciences, and philosophy. In practice, this Christian ideology ends up denying, in the name of the Kingdom, constraints ensuing from long-term situations (for example, the fairly stable existence of international capitalism). It suggests that the ferment of the reign of God always requires us to reject imperfect solutions and adopt radical policies.

This new language, applied to the realm of collective life, gives the illusion of adequately re-defining Christian identity in the contemporary world situation. That, no doubt, accounts for part of its success. Do not misunderstand, however, the meaning of what I object to: I do not to rule out, in principle, radical reforms to the way we organize our collective life. Instead, I question an interpretation of the reign of God which, in my opinion, confuses its present impact with its final impact on human affairs. The present impact of the reign of God is subtler than it will be at the end of time. That is why, in the interim between the resurrection and the second coming of Jesus, Christians need a type of commitment that is expecting not a global victory, but rather a tragic mixture of successes and failures. If we turn down, in that interim, the mediation of a this-worldly ethic to guide this type of commitment, we foster illusions, poor strategic judgment and further disappointments for human hope. We would be maintaining a type of optimism that does not sufficiently integrate the irreducible aspects of the drama of life.

While the four optimistic ideologies that I have presented all disappoint, in the end, those who accept them uncritically, many of these people hold to them just the same and refuse to see clearly their limits. They borrow fragments from one or the other, or they recycle old ideologies to adapt them awkwardly to a new situation. That is how, under Reagan and other leaders of the right, conservatism was transformed into neo-conservatism. Relying on economic theories that are far from being unanimously held by experts, it promotes values like the technological inventiveness of a few people, parsimony and austerity. This hope, almost entirely bereft of dreams, does not have much appeal in the short term for the masses, but, in this tough world, many are prepared to abdicate their ability to judge and are willing to leave things up to their convinced leaders.

In this rather gloomy situation, Christians who criticize ideologies that are flawed with respect to hope have done only half their duty. It is also incumbent upon us to find in our religious heritage convictions that are capable of re-energizing the world's hope. These convictions, which are found in the Bible, would not, however, eliminate ideologies. We will always need ideologies to interpret and give direction to our collective existence in any given phase of our history. As religious convictions operate on a different level than ideologies, their role is to correct and broaden the perspectives that we continually risk getting locked into by ideologies. In a period of disillusionment, recourse to our Christian heritage should stimulate a deeper and more creative approach with respect to hope.

5

Religious Reasons to Hope

The purpose of this chapter is to trace the path for a resurgence of Christian hope in the context of today's world. We will do this in four stages. First, we shall briefly review the current situation regarding hope; then, we shall turn towards the Bible to gather the basic convictions that will guide our reflection; thirdly, we shall point out that while hope can find new life through quality interpersonal relationships, it also encounters at the heart of interpersonal relationships a confrontation with evil; finally, we shall show how Jesus, through his death and resurrection, offers us a radical solution.

The current situation

In our time, the quality of all plant and animal life on our planet, including human life, and even the survival of the human species are threatened. We feel this threat in the context of a world that is at once very organized and yet torn by all sorts of conflicts. The problems we face, then, are complex and serious.

In our world, three main positions stand out. First, we see the optimism of a privileged minority pursuing its arbitrary ambitions, destructive though they might be of the well-being of the world population. While some thirty-five years ago, the middle and lower classes of the industrialized countries were largely associated with prosperity, today far fewer people benefit from the system. The result is a competitive individualism among those trying to earn degrees, find profitable work and succeed professionally. The optimism that is maintained in this way leaves one simultaneously worried about one's own fate and unsympathetic towards the lower rungs of society.

The second position consists of opting out and taking solace in the myriad forms of diversion, in the irrational, a disembodied spirituality, or the afterlife. This is the position taken by most people, including, among others, unemployed people, people on social assistance or those whose jobs are meaningless or low paying. Their attitude is one of pessimism, sometimes coupled with dreams not involving human perseverance, such as winning the lottery.

The third position is that of the creative minorities who take really worthwhile initiatives for a community or for society as a whole. These initiatives are a sign of vitality. They embody a realism in search of motivation and renewal. It is in relation to these creative minorities that we need to envision the movement of a hope seeking justification and revitalization and which goes back to Jesus Christ. They offer, to as many "sheep without a shepherd" as possible, access to the hope that Jesus Christ gives.

Biblical convictions

The Bible reflects a deep hope that goes beyond optimism or pessimism. This hope struggles to improve the lot of humankind while remaining fully aware of the tragic situations that humans must cope with. This hope is not pessimistic, for it observes limited improvements and expects progress to be partial. Nor is it optimistic for, as it is conscious of the heavy weight of the sin of the world, it does not expect the moral and religious advancement of all of humanity.

In the chart below, I have suggested biblical convictions about God, the consequences of these convictions for hope, and attitudes that are incompatible with these convictions. This chart is not meant to be a complete synthesis of Judeo-Christian hope; rather, it offers some foundations that might enable our contemporary hope to find its bearings. I might add that this chart was created in dialogue with the late Viateur Yelle, professor of exegesis at the Institut de pastorale in Montreal.

Convictions	Consequences for hope	Incompatibilities
God, creator of the universe and author of the Torah	Active and harmonious insertion into an ordered world	Arbitrary ambitions
God, who entrusts history to free agents	Stewardship and responsibility for making history	Evasion or neglect of earthly duties
God, Lord of history in partnership with humanity	Meaning to be ascribed to events, trust	Absurdity, despair, fear
God of the incarnation and the resurrection	Faith in human life, solidarity in the face of evil	Disdain for human life, flight in the face of evil
God who saves and whose Spirit acts	Sense of grace, power to love, conversion	Voluntarism or abdication
God, who makes and fulfills promises	Anticipation of the Kingdom	Absolutization of a this-worldly future or of the present

First of all, the faith of Israel confesses God to be creator of the universe and author of the Torah (or of the Law as the path to wisdom and life) and brings about the desire to insert oneself actively and harmoniously into an ordered world. As this world is ordered or structured by the Creator according to a set of coherent relationships, believers renounce arbitrary ambitions. They do not grant themselves the right to dominate nature thoughtlessly or to exploit others. Their attitude of respect towards the environment and towards humanity contrasts with the excesses of modern times and of the present day, when some have wanted to be absolute masters of the earth and have tried to organize it according to their short-term interests, as if they were gods.

The second conviction has to do with a God who entrusts history to free agents. As stewards of a realm that, while belonging entirely to God, is nevertheless entrusted to us, we acknowledge that we are not the owners of this world and we accept the responsibility of making history. This is why the evasion or neglect of earthly duties appears under incompatibilities. It may be interesting to note here what Mircea Eliade wrote, following the Second World War, with respect to this temptation: "It is not inadmissible to think of an epoch, and an epoch not too far distant, when humanity, to ensure its survival, will find itself reduced to desisting from any further 'making' of history...[and] will confine itself to *repeating* prescribed archetypal gestures, and will strive to *forget*, as meaningless and dangerous, any spontaneous gesture which might entail 'historical' consequences."[5]

That God entrusts history to free agents does not mean God remains inactive. In a mysterious manner, God proves to be Lord of history, in partnership with the chosen people and subsequently with all of humanity. This means that these free agents are invited to give a meaning to events and to trust that they all contain potential value, painful and diminishing though they may be. It also means that feelings of meaninglessness, despair, and fear cannot have the last word.

Fourthly, the God of the incarnation and resurrection is present in everything humans experience in the way of love and in the way of evil. Jesus manifests faith in life and engages in solidarity in the face of evil. By raising him from death, God makes this faith and this solidarity victorious in the midst of successes and failures alike. The incredible love of God motivates believers to reject any disdain for human life and not to flee evil. We are called upon to look evil in the face, to fight it, and when inevitable, to accept it in union with Jesus.

Through his Spirit, which acts in the hearts of believers and people of goodwill, God also manifests himself as saviour. The Spirit of the risen Jesus is communicated to humankind and is the source of the grace that comes to us, the power to love that is offered us, and the conversion we are invited to. This experience of a life lived in the Holy Spirit rules out voluntarism—that is, opting to rely solely on one's own power—as well as abdication in the face of ethical and religious challenges.

Finally, the God who makes promises and fulfills them encourages us to anticipate the values and joys of the Kingdom. The realization of these promises is modest during this interim time between Jesus' resurrection and his return in glory. We must therefore not absolutize a future which is restricted to this world and which we would like to see become qualitatively better than the present. On the other hand, hope also excludes any absolutization of the present, any systematic preference for the status quo, or the absence of risk and creativity when it comes to promoting justice and reducing injustice.

The interpersonal challenge of hope

The challenge faced by those who are part of a creative and active minority is not to lose sight of the meaning of their commitment. To succeed at this, the other members of the group—or certain members at least—must reflect this meaning through welcome and support. Communication and solidarity enable one to stay motivated. In interpersonal relations, it is the power of those closest to us that should be emphasized: those with whom we are friends, the partners in a couple, or the members of a family. The experience of real attachment and deep love generates a renewal of hope for persons who are committed in their work and who exercise responsibilities.

The challenge of hope at the heart of interpersonal relationships comes from a hesitation that is directly related to the experience of evil. Every conscious human being realizes that nature, the social system, other people, and even one with whom we share intimately may let us down. Furthermore, we may fail others and even fail ourselves. Looking at the sin of others, one might feel neglected, disrespectfully treated or abandoned, and therefore be sad, indignant, bitter, or discouraged. Looking at one's own sin, one might experience either guilt—that is, disappointment about our own self-depreciation—or a more objective regret when we properly recognize the harm we have done.

Reconciliation with others and with oneself is demanding; the temptation is not to be honest with oneself and to avoid loyal and intimate encounters with others. What is important to note here is that this type of interpersonal problem entails a deterioration of social attitudes. Putting up barriers and withdrawing into oneself diminishes the quality of interpersonal relations even in the work environment or in activities that involve relatively large groups. The joy of attentiveness to others is replaced by excessive self-affirmation, a distancing, indifference, manipulation, and so on. When dissatisfaction and conflict arise, one feels incapable of expressing them adequately and resolving them; one may seek artificial solutions based on giving up or on pressure tactics.

The transparency of hope gives way to the clutter of idols—those values we distort by absolutizing them instead of having them serve the human good. Instead of accepting the interpersonal and social requirements of human reality, these values are used as symbols of the worth that an individual or a group wants assigned to it. We could think of money or success or a thousand and one other symbols of social or professional status. The human being wishes to attribute to itself beauty, goodness, value; we long to be precious in the eyes of those who are significant to us. This may be achieved through honest means or dishonest means: either by receiving esteem in a natural and healthy way, or by extracting it from others through coercion.

This very fundamental problem tests our hope. Behind this terrible awkwardness of idolatry, there is a hidden fear that suffocates hope. How can we explain this multiform fear? In my opinion, it consists in an apprehension of experiencing (or re-experiencing) failure. This experience is painful when it is accompanied, on the one hand, by personal guilt (we falsely accuse ourselves of not being good because we have failed at a particular task or have let an opportunity for good slip by) and, on the other, by blame, discredit, indifference, or rejection coming from others. Essentially, we fear finding meaninglessness, emptiness, and ugliness within ourselves.

This fear destroys human relationships, for it produces a basic distrust, a defensive attitude, and a lack of openness and willingness to take risks. It also plays a big part in the decision not to attempt reconciliation: such a step could lead to awkwardness, misunderstanding, or hurts, as one could easily end up in a weak position. Finally, it could lead one to feel even guiltier. Those who will not take the painful risk of sharing fear that the other person will point a malicious finger at their failings and will bring about in them feelings of stupidity, cowardice or foolishness. Such people rarely venture into the fray; they confine themselves to skirmishes; they do not believe in peaceful negotiation resulting in neither winner nor loser, but only human beings who respect each other. So it is not surprising, then, that a diffuse anxiety quietly erodes their hope.

Towards a radical solution

What I have just described is not far removed from everyday life. What is profound is often very ordinary. Yet it is in our ordinary everyday life that Jesus opens up to us a radical solution as far as hope is concerned. This "solution" does not come about once and for all or effortlessly: it must be breathed into us, so to speak, by the Holy Spirit, who shows us how desirable it is. However, here as elsewhere, there are stages to go through. Once we have got beyond them, that which earlier seemed impossible now seems simple, natural, the only desirable state of mind, because it is the only one that is the source of life.

There is in fact a way of meeting God that makes guilt melt away and loosens the knots of fear. One must leave behind any ambivalence towards God and truly believe that God is love. "God is light and in him [sic] there is no darkness at all" (1 John 1:5). One should not expect to be able to fully integrate this affirmation of faith right away. In fact, for most believers, the basic attitude towards God as Parent is one of ambivalence. Psychoanalysts call it a "love-hate relationship," where both love and hate are felt towards a person who elicits affection while simultaneously frustrating the other who loves her or him. If the word "hate" seems too strong, substitute words like dissatisfaction, resentment, distrust, rebellion, and you may be able to bring into your consciousness a feeling that you normally repress.

Humans have many things to "forgive" God for. The Creator has placed them in a finite world, marked by physical evil, suffering, plodding effort in all spheres (intellectual, moral, psychic, and practical) and finally, death. In this world, we find the harm that comes from others particularly hard to bear. If we call it "sin," we are interpreting it—and rightly so—as due to human freedom. It is difficult to not only accept this Judeo-Christian interpretation, but also internalize it to the point where we are no longer tempted to accuse God of having permitted our unhappiness. When others prevent our desires from being fulfilled, how easy it is to feel cold resentment towards the Creator!

In the face of this ambivalent attitude towards God, just reflecting on the meaning of life and of evil will not suffice to bring about a person's reconciliation with God. What we need to do above all is look at Jesus and recognize in him the God who is present in our experience, where successes and failures are interwoven. Through Jesus, God has entered into solidarity with all that is lived in history and suffers all the evil that strikes humanity. What is more, in God's very heart, there is room—not through imperfection or weakness, but because his vitality is so abundant—for genuine compassion towards those who are wounded by the sin of the world. Finally, by raising Jesus from death and giving his Spirit to Jesus and to all humankind, God is associated powerfully and respectfully with the salvation of the world.

The true depth of human hope is reached when believers decide to "come clean" with God. To do this, they need to discover the choices Jesus made during his prophetic mission and his passion so that, through Jesus, they may see the Father with new eyes. Instead of assuming that they love God and that their images of God are free of ambivalence, they need to ask themselves honestly whether they truly desire to live in relationship with God. In this way, they can explore their guilt and their fear without becoming discouraged. God's positive and loving gaze brings emotional healing, inner peace, and acceptance of reality (so hard on some days and easy on others), as well as a willingness to bring mending and improvement to that reality. This state of mind, which flows from friendship the Father, the Son and the Holy Spirit, fosters acceptance of one's limits, forgiveness, reconciliation, and openness to weakness and misery both in oneself and in others. It thus brings about the religious conditions for the possibility of hope.

6

Human Desire and Love of God

For a treatment of the love relationship that may be established between a human being and God, I could do no better than present the thought of English Benedictine Sebastian Moore. Among his books published by Crossroad in New York, I recommend *The Crucified Jesus Is No Stranger*, which appeared in 1977 (in writing this book the author found his own personal style—concise, vigorous, evocative), *The Fire and the Rose Are One* (his masterpiece, published in 1980, in which he presents his understanding of love in search of reciprocity), *The Inner Loneliness* (which, in 1982, applied his philosophy of love to loneliness, self-awareness and sexuality), *Let This Mind Be in You* (his most structured work, which appeared in 1985 and takes up the themes of desire, the quest for intimacy, guilt, and the experience the disciples were able to have of Jesus living, dying and awakening them to the inner life, beyond his death), and finally *Jesus the Liberator of Desire* (1989), which highlights the transformative liberation of desire by Jesus and some of its cultural implications. In the international journal *Concilium* (No. 156, 1982/6) you will find a good article by Moore, entitled "Death as the Delimiting of Desire," in which the latter phrase actually refers to "the liberation of desire." Other writings by Moore have been published in various books and journals; the *Lonergan Workshop* collection, edited under the direction of Fred Lawrence at Boston College, includes several of them.

Desire

The writings of Sebastian Moore represent, in my view, a successful attempt to express the richness of human affectivity. His reflections bring out a central aspect that the modern western tradition has constantly neglected. If you were to ask the question, "What does it mean to desire someone's presence?" many would answer, "We desire when we feel an emptiness inside us, an unsatisfied need, a void to be filled." Few people would say, "We desire someone's presence from the moment we experience within ourselves a vitality, an intensity, an abundance to be realized with another." And if you were to ask the question, "What does it mean to be good?" many would reply, "Being good consists in not doing harm to others, satisfying their needs, and doing them good." Few would say, "Being good consists of being well, radiating and expressing a love of life, sharing your joy, your interests and your talents with others."

Now, for Moore, to desire and to be good are not simply equivalents of receiving and giving, but are based first and foremost on being well and being content with who we are. In other words, the love we feel for others represents neither a void nor a devotion, but assumes an appreciation for what are, what we have, and what we could have, and blooms into a desire for sharing. Thus, based on this attention to the psychology of love, Moore succeeds in presenting in an original way Thomas Aquinas' ontological conviction that every being is in itself good and desirable. What is original is that Moore approaches this truth from the point of view of self-awareness: for the human being endowed with intelligence and love, to be good means to feel at ease with oneself in relation to others. Everything begins, in fact, with self-esteem, which conditions our relationship with others. The person who lacks self-esteem tries to compensate for this shortcoming and find stimulation, by seeking endless gratifying experiences, regardless of how these might affect others; on the contrary, the person who has self-esteem is delighted to be recognized in the very action by which he enriches others. The first type of person will say, either directly or indirectly, to the person with whom he shares intimacy, "I'm really not worth very much, but if you love me, I won't feel so empty." The second type of person will say, "I know I have value as a person, and so do you. How good it is to be in one another's presence!"

Moore observes that if there is one feeling that every human being wants to have, it is precisely that of feeling at ease with oneself and with others, to be convinced of one's worth, to be recognized and desired. The conviction of one's own worth and desirability allow a person to truly desire and truly love. On the other hand, a sense of being empty or undesirable leads to unstable situations, in which human relations can only be completely askew. Someone who has been deprived of affection will either ask very little from others or else ask them for things that give only artificial satisfaction. If you are not at ease with yourself, you might lose your appetite or perhaps succumb to bulimia. To love fully does not begin with negative feelings towards oneself, but with enthusiasm for certain projects, activities or persons. It begins with one's abundance. This does not correspond in any way to an attitude of self-sufficiency, pride or independence. On the contrary, such attitudes would only show that, deep down, one is full of self-doubt. Actually, people who are open to others, out of their own spontaneity and vitality, are completely aware of their own limitations and how much they stand to gain from others.

The feeling that we are desirable is mediated by others. To demonstrate this in a striking way, Moore considers what takes place when someone is sexually aroused or stimulated by another person. If those who feel stimulated are psychologically healthy, they will find themselves suddenly in touch with all their energy potential. Their multiform ability to enter into relationship gets moving. They feel pleased to establish a relationship with the other through a particular action. This phenomenon is in no way limited to the case of genital arousal. All human relationship that motivates and produces interesting activity obeys this general law that Moore has highlighted. Between parents and children, between teachers and students, between friends of both sexes, between colleagues or co-workers of all walks of life, as soon as a situation allows people to awaken their potential, it must be said that they then actualize their love thanks to the confidence—mostly implicit—that someone else has just shown in them.

This love contains two aspects. It proves to be at the same time love of self and love of the other; it desires the other and it desires to see desire in the other. It is important to note here that this reciprocal desire must not be understood according to the biological model of the need one experiences for an object. In humans, the deep wish of desire is not to take possession of the other, but rather to awaken them to their desire for us. The joy that is specifically human springs forth from the discovery that the other person is enlivened, attracted, and feels well in this interpersonal action. Thus, what we wish to awaken in the other is not a need-desire, but their own feelings of desire and desirability. We rejoice when we feel the intensity of the other as that person awakens to the highest form of desire, namely that of sharing the best of himself with another human being. The author calls this the desire to be oneself *for* others. To be for signifies at the same time giving oneself and being recognized. Observe the extent to which, for Moore, healthy human emotions are neither self-centred nor other-centred, but embrace both these aspects in a dynamic manner. Self-awareness and awareness of others, self-love and love of others, interact naturally and mutually support each other. The aberrations of narcissism do not lead Moore to denigrate self-love. In his view, one must go to the core of what narcissism essentially seeks: to become convinced that we are important in the eyes of another person. This is the only path that leads to exchange, to attitudes that foster the happiness of the other, and to the ability to accept confrontation and to grow because of it. Self-affirmation and affirmation of the other are two aspects of a single reality.

The God-question and the experience of God

Other contemporary authors help us identify the various forms that the God-question takes today. Moore helps us to locate this question in the heart of our most central preoccupation: ourselves. In the first chapters of *The Fire and the Rose Are One*, he begins by showing that happiness does not consist in the absence of worries, but rather in the awareness of one's personal value. As before, Moore states that our deepest desire is to be someone for another person; when that person meets that expectation, a great joy naturally emerges. In the face of this desire and this experience, which at times are very intense, it is normal to wonder about their origin and meaning. In this personalist context, the question, "Just why do I exist, I who am a creature of desire?" makes the problem of my worth as a human being even more fundamental. Moore poses the God-question in a very engaging manner. Through his perspective of human affectivity, he seeks to complement the metaphysical approach, which looks at the origin and meaning of the whole of existence. Despite its undeniable intellectual validity, the metaphysical approach generally doesn't lead anywhere unless the individual who is practising it has asked the same question from a psychological point of view. For those seeking meaning that is capable of engaging them existentially, philosophical considerations dealing with the total of reality appear cold, too vast, even overwhelming. In Moore's work, these considerations have their place, but only briefly and at a second stage, to confirm rationally that the God glimpsed through desire is not an illusion but does indeed correspond to the creator of all that exists.

However, while the metaphysical approach turns out for the most part to be uncertain and disappointing, there are also problems with the psychological approach. Moore stresses the fact that many people refuse to take seriously the question of their importance. They are protecting themselves against the extremes that narcissism may lead to; they think that by believing, they take their desires for reality and create out of thin air a God who is passionately interested in human beings. Moore counters this lofty objection by setting out to prove the existence of a human desire for God. To do so, he relies on a central idea found in Ernest *Becker's The Denial of Death*,[6] Moore accepts Becker's thesis that over against their need to protect their personal value, humans face the inevitability of their death. Becker contends that denying death is a way of rejecting any dependence with respect to a troubling mystery: I have not always existed and I shall leave this world one day. Because this inescapable fact is at odds with the human animal's instinct of self-preservation, Becker maintains that we repress all consciousness of this truth: we deny our dependence and affirm our autonomy; we wish to create ourselves through our projects in order to prove to ourselves that we are important, and to give meaning to our lives. While he accepts what Becker says concerning the denial of death, the search for personal value that is manifested in this denial makes sense to Moore. He understands clearly that during one's short earthly life, one may reject the troubling mystery of the apparent nothingness from which we come and to which we return. On the other hand, he dares to ask the question, "What if the fact that I am passionately interested in myself found its meaning and its fulfillment in the discovery that I am important to this mystery from which I originate?"

This question illustrates the difference between Becker and Moore. Becker falls into the widespread contradiction which consists of speaking intelligently about human life as being, in the final analysis, *absurd;* Moore realizes that following the quest for meaning through to the end assumes we affirm there is a purpose to the fundamental desire which constitutes the unique character of the human. As Moore explains, Becker thinks that the human animal should pursue meaning by rejecting the idea of dependence on the troubling mystery. It did not occur to him that this mystery could be something other than a threat to the provisional and precarious security of the human self. Moore, on the contrary, sees in this dependence, which is itself subject to mystery, the meaning we so ardently seek. With a view to this dependence becoming acceptable, he asks himself honestly how to characterize this mystery.

Moore resumes the analysis of desire and identifies a depth of desire that allows us to speak of God in a manner that is both rationally rigourous and emotionally rich. As I mentioned above, it is a matter of demonstrating that a human desire for God exists. At the beginning of *The Inner Loneliness*, Moore points out the paradox of inner loneliness: the very thing in me that prompts me to enter into relationship seems condemned never to be shared. No one would be able to feel that sense I have of being special, unique, and priceless, exactly as I feel it within me. Now, this sense that I have—which goes right through my awareness of my limitations—of having, despite everything, an irreplaceable value, is not an illusion. Moore draws our attention to the indignation and anger that rise up in any psychologically healthy person when they are ignored, left out, discredited or looked upon with disdain. If the feeling of self-value that every sensible person has is an illusion, how shall we explain the impression we have so spontaneously that the denial of this value is unjust and unacceptable? But if, on the one hand, this feeling is not an illusion and if, on the other, no other person can share it completely, are we not in the presence of a human desire for God? Is there not, in the depths of the human heart, a longing—no doubt hesitant, but nonetheless real—to be totally understood and loved in the most precious thing we have received? Certainly, most of the time this desire remains unarticulated. Moreover, one must not imagine that it is a substitute for inter-human desire. On the contrary, when it is experienced in a positive way, the desire for God enhances the quality and intensity of interpersonal relationships.

Moore explains the two faces of desire—inter-human desire and the desire for God—in the following manner. Let us remember what we have already seen, namely, the inter-human face of desire. In the experience of being attracted to a person, value or project, desire comes from that sense of being desirable which is awakened and stirred up through the mediation of what attracts me. There are three terms here:

one's desirability | the fact of desiring | that which is desired

The person, the value, or the project that is desired constitutes the intermediary that, from an external source, activates my desirability, that is to say, that potential for well-being, self-esteem, and esteem for others which produces the fact of my desiring. In relation to this three-part scheme, what is the other face of desire? It is a desire with no particular object, which many people feel without understanding its full significance. In this case, the third term—that which is desired—is absent. The experience consists of just wanting, of experiencing one's desirability without mediation, of feeling at ease while desiring without desiring anything in particular. From the perspective of the inter-human face of desire, one perceives one's own desirability *indirectly* through the mediation of that which is desired (or, more intensely, of the person who is desired). From the perspective of the human-divine face of this same desire, one perceives one's own desirability *directly* and it is activated from within, without any intermediary. This is the philosophical structure of the affective experience of God.

Identifying the incomparable Being who awakens and confirms our own desirability from within may be relatively easy for some people. In general, however, our openness to God is characterized by ambivalent feelings. Moore observes that we can be thoroughly in love with the Source of our being and at the same time have hostile feelings towards this Source. Due to all the evil which, on this earth, opposes our own desirability, it is quite normal, in the course of our religious journeying, that we might be internally divided towards our Creator. Moore clarifies this itinerary by distinguishing two major phases. During the first phase, the individual experiences a nostalgia for this Being who would confirm one's personal value in a definitive way. In the second phase, the individual mysteriously hears the answer that was both hoped for and unhoped for. I believe that the ineffable joy and meaning felt during the second phase do much to reduce the ambivalence and to intensify the positive feelings towards God.

Moore brings out in a completely original way the God-question and the experience of God. In contrast to many other Christian authors who do not treat the subject of desire in sufficient depth, he does not content himself with saying that the encounter with God is similar to an interpersonal encounter. By not going beyond this parallel, these authors do not show how the approach and the discovery of God provide an over-abundance of meaning and joy, and even a fullness of meaning and joy that cannot be found in human relationships. By identifying the God-question and specifying what the experience of God consists of, Moore has rendered theology and religious psychology an invaluable service.

Guilt and sin

The more often someone experiences the fulfillment of one of his desires, the more he knows the meaning, scope, and limit of this desire. One who loves knows a lot more about love than one who does not love. But in this domain, pure extremes are rare. No one stands completely in the light or completely in the dark. We cannot fail to be struck by the twilight in which we all find ourselves before the great realities of desire, love, and human relations. Here is where Christianity has a unique contribution to offer, given its lengthy preoccupation with the problem of loving and the problem of evil. In order to present Christian convictions on this subject in a meaningful way, Moore starts out from what psychoanalysis teaches concerning guilt. His philosophy of desire enables him to be innovative and to put forward elucidations that go beyond the discoveries of Freud.

Phenomenologically speaking, it is easy to observe that the opposite of self-love is the shame the self feels when it inflates itself and acts to attract attention. At the time, it experiences elation, even euphoria, but soon after, along with the disappointment in oneself, comes discontent, and depression. While so many Christian thinkers have denounced this ego-inflation without understanding it, Moore sees in this recurring cycle of euphoria/depression the problem of a self-love that is poorly adjusted and unsure of itself, and painfully trying to find itself. He sees in this awkward self-affirmation a lack of self-confidence and even a self-hate that drives this quest for love towards repeated failures. Far from pointing to an excess of self-love, his diagnosis is a deficiency in self-love. He rightly considers this deficiency as the main cause of the moral chaos created by individuals who lack love. Because they do not respect themselves as much as their Creator does, and because they denigrate themselves either openly or secretly, these people are afraid to invest the best of themselves in their relations with others and pursue instead all kinds of superficial and harmful effects.

Moore observes in the humans a curious resistance to their own desirability. This resistance is explained, in part, by the guilt inevitably felt in the way we experience freedom. During childhood, the wishes of adults generally held sway: by complying, the child often repressed its own self-love. A conflict then developed between the expression and the control of one's desire. Learning control allowed the child to avoid being opposed by adults and to guarantee its own safety. Ever since then, each time we affirm our desire in a way that does not correspond to the expectations of those around us, we feel guilty. As Erich Fromm explains in *Man for Himself*,[7] guilt appears as soon as an individual breaks loose from his surroundings and acts independently. Even if his behaviour is morally irreproachable, he will feel he is in the wrong from the standpoint of the social or family norms that he contradicts. This aspect of guilt is not just about moral fault: it is the feeling that accompanies the idea of doing things our own way, starting our own business, so to speak, thinking for ourselves, and following our own judgment rather than the traditional wisdom absorbed during our years of socialization.

This first form of guilt, which Moore calls childhood guilt and which lasts well beyond childhood if not all one's life, is not the most important one. There is a second form of guilt, which the author calls adult guilt and which is not to be understood in connection with the affirmation of one's freedom, but rather in connection with the relational character of the human being. It is the feeling that results from the fact that one has failed another human being, that one has not given that person what he is entitled to, that one has not responded to his call or to his love. This feeling is one and the same as the feeling of having failed ourselves, that is, having failed that which in ourselves desires relationship and exchange. The wrong that is thus committed—or, in religious language, the sin—consists not only of a wrong done to another. On a deeper level, it is that we are submitting to the part of ourselves that is afraid to love; that we are blocking this source of life that could have poured forth from us towards others. To do wrong is just as much an attack on oneself as on others. It is the most regrettable misunderstanding that could occur: renouncing one's deeper self in favour of a superficial, artificial self, anxious for power and control, that flees authentic human relations. This may well happen without causing any serious external harm. It is enough to suppress in ourselves a certain capacity to listen, to respond with generosity, to invest our actions with sincere interiority. Moore points out that a good deal of this suppression is done unconsciously: simply not appreciating this part of oneself is to weaken it and, in the long run, seriously damage it. Sometimes we say about someone, "That person has no heart." We are referring to a hardness of heart, but the expression applies equally to those who anaesthetize or try to neutralize their heart. They are really the first victim of their misguidedness. Their victimization is all the worse because they never manage to rid themselves completely of their desire to love and be loved. One would have to say they are wounded and wounding hearts.

Sin consists then of ratifying our tendency to flee authentic and committed relationships with others. But where does this tendency come from? To reply to this question, Moore consults both genetic psychology and the Judeo-Christian doctrine of original sin. He describes first of all the two principal crises in the development of a child's personality. He cites the work of Margaret Mahler[8] to show how decisive the first crisis—which spans especially the first two years of life—is. The very young must, indeed, learn to deal with their individuality. A child's mother sometimes or, perhaps even often (as the case may be), gives mixed messages that cause anxiety: "Either stick with me or tough it out on your own!" Because parents are never perfectly clear, it is impossible for the child always to receive exactly the right degree of support and encouragement to enable it to assume its individuality harmoniously. The second crisis, the Oedipus complex, brought to light by Freud, is better known. Coming later than the first, it focuses on the separation of the boy or girl from the parent of the opposite sex. Once again, the child must repress its desire, which becomes the id. The child must accept a self defined by the roles appropriate to his or her sex, and must finally deal with the superego (the Ueber-Ich, the over-the-self) constituted by the parent of the same sex, who forbids total intimacy with the parent of the other sex.

What is the most important consequence of these two crises? While, according to Mahler, children fall in love spontaneously with everything in existence, they learn to control, even repress, this love as they grow up. The constraints they undergo lead them to doubt their own desirability. The failures they register drive them to resent their desire; soon they are accusing their desire of putting them in situations that make them suffer. As they have the impression that it is their self-love that is making them want things that are harmful, they learn to distrust their own inclination and they feel guilty even for loving themselves. In the extreme, if the circumstances have been particularly adverse, they feel hatred and disgust for the best in themselves: their ability to love, to be loved, and to enjoy this love. This is how the child damages its own desirability.

Let us summarize, so we may go further. The first form of guilt comes from the emergence of the self, of that individuality that detaches itself from the maternal breast, then from the family, and then from society. This guilt, which the author calls "childhood guilt"—I would add "and adolescent"—may trigger the will to affirm one's independence in a way that is disrespectful of others. This constitutes sin insofar as this type of affirmation of self, which hurts others, is free. The second form of guilt, called "adult," takes us even more directly into the heart of the human drama. It derives from failure in the face of the possibility of love; it arises from the non-response or inadequate response to the offer of an interpersonal relationship that would have deserved to be established or developed. Here too, there is only sin if the non-response is voluntary. We might wonder, "How could such non-response be voluntary and free?" I think we must affirm that it is, while at the same time admitting that we cannot understand why sin exists. Sin is precisely that which has no reason to exist. While the conditions that foster deviant behaviour can be explained, the decision itself that constitutes sin remains unintelligible and irrational. Following Thomas Aquinas and Bernard Lonergan, Moore stresses the absurd nature of sin: to refuse that which is good, to prefer non-value over a value which would deserve to exist, to repudiate what God would wish to create through us. Mysterious prerogative of humans, capable of not loving because they are capable of loving freely!

The author also talks about original sin. Looking at the third chapter of Genesis, he does not accept the frequently given interpretation that, after the breach with God, sexuality was the first thing to rebel against the spirit. He states, on the contrary, that it was the spirit that began to distrust sexuality. "Then the eyes of both were opened, and they knew that they were naked; and they sewed fig leaves together and made loincloths for themselves" (Genesis 3:7). The shame that made them cover themselves was a sudden awareness that came from their human intelligence, which had become confused following the breach with its Source of intelligibility. In other words, the ego that asserts itself against God begins to assert itself against its own sexuality, the locus par excellence of desire. Then this sexuality fights back against a self that is no longer hospitable to it. At this juncture in his thought, Moore becomes prophetic. He denounces a major current in the West that has influenced many people both inside and outside Christianity. He calls it the voice of sin. It is the voice of the sinning ego that casts blame on God as well as on sexuality. This voice declares, "Life and death teach me that I must not take my desires for real. The only reality I can accept is whatever I can acquire in this life (some would add: and in the next) through my control over my self and others." This voice is the voice of the ego that represses its desire and refuses to be open to the deeper self. Note that it is Jung's distinction between the "ego" and the "self" that the author is following. In non-technical language, let us say that the ego is the equivalent of the personality, with clearly defined characteristics and limits, which directs one's actions and shapes one's destiny; the self, however, corresponds to a broader area encompassing the ego and to which the ego can have access if it agrees to be led, in a disconcerting manner, by forces that transcend it. Now, the voice of the ego, which opposes the self, is the voice of sin. By attacking sexuality, it attacks not only sexuality as a symbol of desire, but also desire itself which, by nature, is open to God.

This rejection of desire turns out to be present in a great number of believers and non-believers alike—whether their belief or non-belief is theoretical or practical. In all people who opt for an ego that is closed to deep desire, the voice of sin speaks of resignation in the face of a "reality" viewed from the perspective of power and control. In this regard, the reversal that Moore shows us is that in the witness and discourse of many Christians the voice of sin is disguised as the voice of original sin. While this doctrine, true in itself, designates the alienating situation that God wants to liberate us from, the voice of sin takes over this doctrine and declares, "You will never see the end of your desire, but try to curb your desire and, by doing so, you will earn eternal life." In the context of our earthly existence, this is categorically the voice of despair. It does not take seriously the grace of the Holy Spirit, the Father's will to save us, and the resurrection of Jesus, the decisive character of which, here in this life, is proclaimed throughout the entire New Testament—even though their effects are still incomplete. In fact, this voice denies the liberating impulse of desire which starts right here and now. Thus, if our Christianity is authentic, it obeys the voice of the Holy Spirit; if it is inauthentic, it obeys the voice of sin. To the extent that Christianity has listened to the voice of the ego closed in on itself, it has simply reflected the male culture of modern times, disrespectful of nature, desire, and the feminine alike.

Moore's understanding of desire is completely opposite to the narrow, prevailing Western understanding. For him, desire, like intelligence, consists of a dynamic that is essentially open; some contemporary philosophers would call it an intentionality. On the other hand, this intentionality may be artificially limited, due to widespread prejudices. Moore presents the psychological as well as the religious ramifications of this undue limiting of desire. The connection he discovers between non-openness to desire and non-openness to God is most remarkable. By rejecting, for understandable but disastrous psychological reasons, the consequences of a desire that would follow itself through to the end, we reject the call of that Totality which makes its presence known in the heart of our desire. The ego, which does not want to die, rejects the transformation into a vaster self. Original sin, which remains incomprehensible, consists of refusing the risks of one's desirability and, thus, closing oneself off from the true God.

Salvation discovered in Jesus

Sebastian Moore has always been fascinated by Jesus. All his life, he wanted to take seriously the salvation offered by Jesus Christ, asking himself how to talk about it without talking through his hat. Inspiration came to him in a country church near Rome, on the feast of the Sacred Heart, while the first antiphon of Vespers was being sung: "One of the soldiers pierced his side with a spear, and at once blood and water came out" (John 19:34). Moore comments: "Quietly and in a part of the mind that does not wrestle with concepts, I knew that the whole thing was there: the act of aggression, of sin, releasing the waters of grace."[9] Everything was there in this very pregnant vision, but it would have to be seen in relation to central aspects of lived human experience in order to be described in a meaningful way. Thus, when considering Jesus, Moore concentrates on a place of interaction between Jesus and any person interested in Jesus. What is that place? It is the place of our fundamental human experience, submitting to the challenge of becoming illuminated and transformed upon contact with Jesus. This is why the things Moore says about desire, the God-question, the pre-Christian experience of God, guilt, and sin are so important. Moore's reflections can be seen as a creative transposition for our time of the method of interaction between Christ and the meditating believer that Ignatius of Loyola developed in the context of sixteenth-century culture. Moreover, the thirty-day Ignatian Spiritual Exercises, in which Moore engaged in 1971, marked a turning point in his life.

Moore offers us an original approach to the Jesus Christ event. With respect to his life and death, he distinguishes the point of view held by Jesus' adversaries and that of his disciples. His adversaries succeed in doing away with him. Why? The common explanation states that Jesus had become a threat to the political and religious establishment in Jerusalem. Moore does not reject this real factor. But his psychological construct helps us reach a deeper level of understanding, as it can throw light upon our own personal attitudes. If the Roman and Jewish authorities of the day attacked Jesus, it was because when they discovered the extraordinary human quality of Jesus, they reacted with fear and animosity. It was the kind of quality that contrasts with the dullness of everyday life and makes us feel all the more that we are just struggling along. In Jesus, they could see that heart full of life and generosity that they had repressed, not without effort, in themselves. The confrontation with a prophet who lived his desirability deeply and was in constant relationship with a fatherly and merciful God was a reproach to all those who had pledged their loyalty to a narrow-minded and fastidious socio-religious regime. Some of the leaders of Israel gave in to a dangerous resentment towards Jesus, a resentment that consists of the veiled hostility that is felt upon seeing the goodness and generosity of someone better than us. Those who had resigned themselves to sin, guilt, and death, and who had disguised their resignation in the trappings of a literalist faithfulness to God's law, could not stand the liberating message of Jesus.

Despite how destructive it was, the experience of Jesus' enemies remains superficial, for it was confined to a rather vague understanding of desire, sin and guilt. On the contrary, in the disciples who witnessed Jesus' preaching, awareness of these realities was pushed to an extreme by the fact that they lived with a master whose desire was uninhibited, who had neither sin nor guilt: the beloved of the Father. In Galilee, because of Jesus, they experienced their desirability as well as the love of God with an incomparable intensity. Through the intermediary of Jesus, who brought their desire to an indescribable peak, they had a very deep experience of God, which stimulated their hope tremendously. And yet, this hope was disappointed, as we learn from the disciples at Emmaus in Luke 24:19-21. In Jesus' death, the voice of sin was heard and appeared final. So, sin, guilt, isolation, and death had won out over love, meaning, and desire! Where Jesus himself had failed no one else could succeed. After Jesus, there was no more reason to hope. On Good Friday, the disciples were completely distraught and broken.

Moore's emphasis on the final failure of this mediation with God that the disciples had experienced in Jesus must be seen in relation to the fact that one can be awakened to one's own desirability either from within or without. During the life of Jesus, the disciples came to their desirability *from without*, being led to it by their friendship with Jesus. By contrast, Moore interprets the presence of the risen Jesus as calling the disciples *from within* to recover their desirability, which they had lost when Jesus was captured and put to death. Since only God can thus awaken human beings, without an intermediary, to their own loving vitality, Moore points out that in doing so Jesus exercises a function that is specifically divine. The post-resurrection appearances of Jesus, on the experiential level, constitute the first steps towards the recognition of his divinity.

In this confrontation with the risen Jesus, believers have an experience of God that fully integrates the facets of evil represented by death, sin, and guilt. The presence of Jesus alive after his death may not be fundamentally different from the experience of God that we presented earlier without mentioning Jesus, for they both involve the action of the Holy Spirit in the human heart. Yet the encounter with Jesus Christ is more complete than the pre-Christian encounter with God because it does not exclude any dimension of the human condition. Only that encounter can, in fact, reveal how far the negation of the self and of others can go: it can go so far as to attack the life of God offered in Jesus. Nowhere is the power of sin so evident as in the vision of the just person condemned, the innocent victim, the lamb that is slain. At the same time, thanks to Jesus' resurrection, that is to say, thanks to a situation reversal that is purely divine and beyond our comprehension, the cross of Jesus becomes the opportunity for repentance. In Moore's view, the crucifixion should not provoke guilt (the general impression of being at fault) or regret (specific acknowledgment of what should have been done differently) so much as sorrow. The sorrow felt flows from discovering that the interpersonal relationship itself (and not just a particular action) is amiss. The wounded and wounding heart realizes that it has wounded itself and that it has wounded God by wounding others. In connection with this salutary realization, sorrow opens the person who experiences it to the possibility of a new relationship with the other. When this other who forgives is the risen Jesus, a unique kind of hope is offered. Confronted by God who, in the person of Jesus, eliminates our sin and restores our desirability, guilt loses its power. More precisely, what vanishes is the guilt perpetuated by sin, which consists of refusing the desirability of God and our own, and which projects a shadow onto God, a shadow of darkness and hostility. The impact of the resurrection consists in this: that the Holy Spirit invites us to let ourselves find new life, to transcend the boundaries of the ego, to recognize that the love manifested in the life, death, and post-resurrection appearances of Jesus can re-create our desire, open it fully to the divine project and engage it, in a mystical way, in the establishment of more humanizing relationships and social structures.

Part III

PASTORAL DISCERNMENT

7

Three Mentalities Faced by the Churches

For 2000 years now, there has been uninterrupted dialogue, some-times slow moving, sometimes fast-paced, between Christianity itself and the cultures through which it is expressed. Throughout this process, alert Christians have questioned prevailing attitudes in their era and have endeavoured to respond in a manner that is both open and critical. In the hope of making a small contribution to this dialogue, I shall present here three major mentalities in the Western world, which I have called empirical, psychological and spiritualistic. I shall briefly describe the basic concern of each of these mentalities and point out how each of them influences the way people, Christians included, think and live today. I shall also make some pastoral sugges-tions regarding the directions and emphases that the churches should undertake in view of these mentalities.

The empirical mentality

This mentality began to assert itself in the seventeenth century with the systematic application of the scientific method. It is very widespread among those who attend university and study the natural and human sciences. The empirical approach is not confined to the realm of the sciences but is quite naturally transposed to morality and to one's philosophy of life. It dismisses ideologies, as these did not live up to the expectations they raised (for example, behaviourism in education and Marxism in politics and in unionism). It does not trust theories: it judges ideas by how practical they are and judges practices by how effective they are. When this mentality is superficial, it de-generates into "technologism," which revels in technology's prowess and is ready to undertake anything it is materially capable of. On the other hand, when this mentality is at its best, it is critical in the face of technology's ambiguous results. When enlivened by a moral sense that pays attention to the consequences of decisions by those in authority, the empirical mentality can choose an ecological, anti-nuclear stance and show concern for the plight of the poor in first- and third-world countries alike.

With respect to culture and religion, the empirical mentality emphasizes reasons for living as well as right action. It does not easily accept truths it does not see as making sense. How can it test concretely the value or meaning of paradoxical Christian ideas such as non-violence, forgiveness or the cross? Aware that history is more or less relative, it is sceptical when churches claim they possess absolute truth. Judeo-Christian revelation thus appears as one revelation among others and loses its status of revelation in the strict sense. Without being completely closed to the idea of a God who would be accessible and would speak to human beings, many people wonder about the validity of his mediators throughout history and about the credibility of those who present themselves as his current spokespersons. Moreover, they have the impression (whether justified or not) that Christianity has shown less wisdom and respect for people than have other religious traditions.

Since an empirical mindset is stymied by questions of truth but is interested in practical results, churches should endeavour to be places where problems of moral and religious authenticity can be explored. Catholicism in particular has spiritual and ethical discernment criteria to offer that can answer—and even fully satisfy—the queries of sincere persons who are wondering about the right use not only of method but also of religious traditions. Catholicism also has many past and present witnesses who manifest, in their lives and in their commitment, the fruits of the Gospel. The churches must first of all respond to this concern for ethical and religious verification, which the empirical mentality promotes. Having satisfied this existential requirement, it will be easier to help people today to move beyond their pragmatic and relativist horizon. It is a matter, then, of making the connection between the Gospel experience and truth. How is this done? First, it needs to be shown that a courageous living out of the Gospel must be supported by true convictions. Secondly, it must be shown that God has made it possible for us to access these true convictions by inspiring the prophets through his Holy Spirit, and by making Jesus, his Son, known to us.

The psychological mentality

Just as medicine gave birth to the hope of better health, and just as science and technology gave rise to great expectations of material progress, so psychology created in our contemporaries the desire for improvement in the way we function as individuals and in the way we relate to one another. Many people try to look at their problems: they try to find ways to become more independent; they seek inner harmony and good communication with others; they are concerned about their bodies, the food they eat, how they spend their leisure time; they seek balance in their interests and in how they use their time and energy. However, given the precarious and sometimes even ambiguous and disappointing results of psychotherapy and personal growth sessions, the fragility of this search for liberation is keenly felt and one becomes open to religion—on the condition that there is no anti-psychological morality involved.

Christians are influenced by the psychological mentality. Many have given up any strict observance of the law, embarking instead on a quest for human authenticity marked by a certain freedom and ease in the way they function and in their interpersonal relationships. Moral imperatives focus less on what one must do than on how one must do it. We also have a certain flair for recognizing and appreciating attitudes that denote love of one's neighbour and that foster life and make us more human.

Confronted by this mentality, the churches have a challenge to meet, namely to develop pastoral attitudes that involve greater empathy, intuition and respect for the reflection and the decision-making that individuals are engaged in. When it is necessary for Christians to confront and question others, they must do so by relating to the best in people, that is, their reason, their conscience, and their desire to understand and to be motivated. Christian accompaniment also consists of helping people to discover the psychological causes of their shortcomings and to envisage these as the expression of a quest for meaning that is searching in the wrong places. This accompaniment also assumes an emphasis on fundamental morality (rather than on isolated acts, separated from their existential context), rooted in theological truth.

The spiritualistic mentality

This mentality includes extremely varied and uneven spiritual interests: astrology, tarot cards, dreams and religious experiences, fortune-telling, and exceptional powers, sects, gnosis, meditation groups, psychology-and-spirituality therapy groups, and so forth. It seems these interests affect all layers of North American society, although very differently depending on culture and social class. What is important to note is that we can get a faint glimpse here of a dimension that transcends scientific and technological rationality. It represents a search for confidence and serenity amidst the uncertainty of events. This mixed bag of a movement also has an apocalyptic wing, serving as a vehicle of self-expression for a generation of young people who have been very much affected by the drug culture and by the nuclear threat.

It seems to me that despite the importance of this mentality, many priests and lay Christians hardly understand it. Is this because they are being loyal to a personalism that focuses on human relations, and because their reading of the Bible is limited to one where the word sheds light on the meaning of everyday life? To the extent that this is true, we must regret this overly comfortable vision of Christianity, which is not very open to the irrational side, to the wounds life inflicts, and finally to the salvation offered by Jesus Christ. On the contrary, one may find in many so-called charismatic Christians, for example, a spiritualistic tendency that gives great importance to miracles, to emotional healing, to a certain fusion with God and with the group of believers, as well as to apocalyptic anticipation of terrible social calamities.

To meet the needs of people of this type, the churches must be more hospitable and develop a richer array of symbols that can touch people's minds and hearts. It must emphasize the relationship between God and individuals in distress. People also need spiritual guides who can show them practical paths to union with God: the current renewal in the spiritual life and in modes of prayer is meeting this expectation. Likewise, many places of worship and many religious movements have re-thought their pastoral vision so as to be in creative fidelity to the orientation given by the Second Vatican Council and in order to respond to the searching that popular religion represents. Finally, faced with the difficult task of purifying a faith in which an infantile religiosity has become entrenched, where does one turn? One must rely on a sound philosophy, a theology that stays close to the spiritual life, and a psychological and moral wisdom inspired by the best of what society has to offer in these fields. At the same time, these approaches must be situated within a Gospel context, where they may be corrected or extended as necessary.

8

Evoking, Discerning and Extending the Experience

In these early years of the twenty-first century, the religious expectations of post-industrial societies are numerous. Many Christians, first of all, demonstrate a thirst for spirituality, prayer, adoration, mystical involvement, or a need to internalize the word of God and to taste the great mysteries of our faith. Secondly, psychological and interpersonal preoccupations accompany this spiritual search: people desire achievement and find themselves striving towards the harmonious realization of their identity as a human person; they admit they are seeking a Source capable of fulfilling their spiritual aspirations; and they are also discovering that experiences of community, sharing and friendship lead to this Source. Thirdly, they want the inspiration to be able to make courageous social choices, or they desire the certainty of being loved, to buoy them up in moments of suffering or darkness.

Faced with this triple expectation—of a felt discovery of the mystery and beauty of God, a discovery embodied in a psychological search and in interpersonal encounters, and which fosters a fuller commitment to the struggle of life—I would like to describe briefly a mode of pastoral presence which consists of evoking, discerning and extending the religious experience.

Evoking

A pastoral approach that aims to serve religious experience must first and foremost offer places where religious experience can be evoked. Being a sort of presence to a dimension of our lives that transcends us, religious experience cannot be expressed or articulated in everyday utilitarian language. On the contrary, it seems to me that this experience can only be evoked, that is, suggested, by a language endowed with poetic value. Only poetic language is capable, in fact, of referring us, through suggestion, to the paths that lead to God. Only poetic language can provide the tone where our respect for the sacred emerges quite naturally; this tone prepares us to become aware once again that our hearts and minds open onto the Mystery and that we are in the amazing presence of an incomparable Presence.

This poetic language does not necessarily require the involvement of professional artists or poets. Nor is it necessary—or even desirable—for the entire liturgy to be imbued with such language. It is sufficient to allow the words, gestures, music, and decor to help us internalize either a significant aspect of our own human experience or the word of God as it is proclaimed and explained. In this way, for example, moments of complete silence in community can be a powerful source of unity focusing our attention on communion with Someone who is supremely important for each of us.

One might object that there is a danger here of falling into aesthetics, that is to say, seeking beauty for its own sake, and to revel in the pleasant feelings or impressions. To do so would be to risk leaving aside the ethical demands of the Gospel.

I will come back later to this real danger, when I talk about extending the religious experience. For now, I want to stress that Christian conversion itself needs to be supported by a poetic language which sets out before the believer the beauty of what God is offering them. To be able to respond with enthusiasm, balance, and joy to the call of Jesus, one needs to have been captivated by the depth of his message and by the magnitude of the love he offers us. Now, it is precisely one of the functions of liturgy—whether it is experienced in a small or a large group—to express symbolically a dimension of our existence that transcends us. In this and other regards, moreover, liturgy is not that different from the Bible itself.

Discerning

It is not enough, however, for religious experience to be evoked through symbolism: it must also be discerned in our lived experience. If we were to content ourselves with being present in an artistic mode to the depth of our humanity with its window on the Infinite, we would risk missing the point that it is not only in events of explicitly religious import, but most often in ordinary perceptions, that God reveals a facet of his mystery. We therefore need guides to help us identify that which has been or could become an occasion of religious experience in our everyday lives. Indeed, our religious experiences normally remain partly unconscious. They are events that we experience with varying degrees of intensity and that allow us to sense something magnificent that is beyond us. But as we are accustomed to finding God only at traditional times and in traditional places—such as the sacraments, personal prayer, life's trials and nature—we hardly know how to recognize God's presence in situations that we think are "just human." Yet experiences we call secular or purely psychological (for example, the search for personal identity, the incomplete realization of values that we hold dear, the quest for meaning, loneliness, openness to communication and intimacy, suffering and joy, ageing and death, and so forth) frequently constitute the mediation through which the Spirit of God speaks to our most intimate selves.

One of the greatest services the Christian community can render today is to become a gathering place where some of the thousand and one current forms of religious experience can be identified. It is simply a matter of expressing them and interpreting them in the light of what Jesus himself lived. Not with the idea of delighting in them or trying to impress one another, but in order to find ways of strengthening our faith and reasons to give thanks. The church can become once again, in today's cultural context, a place of spiritual wisdom and discernment—that is, if it listens more consistently to the many ways the Spirit is calling us through human experiences of religious significance. For this recognition to be fruitful, however, the church must note carefully the difference between an experience that is egocentric or has a sectarian tendency, and an experience that leads to a truly loving attitude. It is the Christian community's contemplation of the person of Jesus and their meditation on his words that allows them to move from an understanding of the divine that might be psychologically questionable and theologically superficial, to the discovery of God as revealed in Jesus. In this way, the community can manifest and deepen the most authentic religious experience, one in which our thirst is quenched by the Font of love.

Extending

The task of discerning religious experience turns out to be inseparable from that of extending it into our daily life. Indeed, religious
experience only becomes and remains authentic if it produces visible
fruit. "You did not choose me but I chose you. And I appointed you
to go and bear fruit, fruit that will last" (John 15:16). Given the fact
of the incarnation, encountering Jesus makes it possible for us to have
a certain quality of presence for others. Properly directed religious
experience, in the long run, gives us emotional inner peace and at the
same time supports us in the unavoidable struggle we must engage in
to see clearly within ourselves and in our relations with others.

This means that the pastoral approach does not need to naïvely
bless, without any critical judgment, any kind of religious experience
whatsoever. On the one hand, the pastor will be aware that many
imperfect paths may lead to God and that religiosity, together with
a sense of the profoundness of the human, creates the intimate space
where the Spirit calls a person who is searching for the fullness of life.
On the other hand, however, the pastor must be convinced that the
long process of conversion and transformation required to maintain
a living relationship with the true God is not simply being bypassed.
That is why I think it is essential that a sound pedagogy of religious
experience should frequently stress the essential link that exists between the spiritual life and interpersonal and social commitment. It
is absolutely necessary to foster a constant flow between prayer and
daily serving one's sisters and brothers. It is on this condition that
religious experience becomes a resource that allows one to engage in
the struggle of life in a manner that is both more peaceful and more
perceptive.

Implementing the kind of pastoral care that fosters a deepening
of the spiritual life represents a huge challenge not only for priests,
but also for the other members of Christian communities. It requires
everyone to be open to a religious experience that is internalized and
becomes increasingly authentic. Planning liturgies capable of evoking the depth dimension of human life demands creative hard work,
inspired by a hunger for beauty and a sense of the sacred. The discernment and the expression of religious experience require that we pay
attention to our lives, that we be psychologically accurate in describing

situations or events we remember, and that we be theologically precise in relating this experience to the meaning of life revealed in the risen Jesus. Finally, extending the encounter with God into everyday life assumes that we are familiar with the milieu we are addressing, that we understand the cultural factors that contribute to shaping it, and that we maintain a passionate concern for the well-being and integrity of all those in our care.

9

Interiority and Relationality

I n Canada, as in most of the highly industrialized countries, an
impressive wave of mysticism has reached broad layers of the
population in the last few decades. In addition to those movements which are specifically Christian and focused on conversion or
prayer, an initiation into spiritual experience is offered by masters
from backgrounds as diverse as psychology, yoga, transcendental
meditation, gnosis, the occult, astrology, and even the drug culture. In
most Montreal bookstores, for example, the sections devoted to these
subjects are much more extensive than those containing traditional
spirituality and theology. It is clear that many of our contemporaries
are discovering their interiority by coming from a perspective appar-
ently quite different from the Christian one.

Despite the divergence in viewpoints that exists between the spirituality of the Gospel, on the one hand, and psychological, gnostic,
or Eastern spiritualities, on the other, it is important to note several
anthropological concepts that they have in common. Furthermore,
movements that call themselves Christian are capable of distortion,
given that we all share the same human nature wounded by the original
alienation. Therefore, it could be useful to consider all these frame-
works of spiritual experience together, regardless of whether they are
labelled as humanist or Christian, and to apply to all of them the same
criteria of authenticity inspired by the Gospel. In doing so, the aim
is in no way to show disdain for or to reject any group whatsoever,
since we Christians cannot escape the aberrations due to sin, and since
it is always in our interest to let ourselves be questioned by our own
spiritual tradition, which derives from the Bible and has been deepened
by 2000 years of experience as church.

Our principal criterion will be the following: any spiritual experience open to a genuine relationship with God, whatever name is given

to God, is authentic. We shall apply this criterion successively to three major problems of interiority, namely, the role of our feelings, embodiment in reality, and the challenge of duration. As each of these aspects offers the possibility of a genuine relationship with the Transcendent, we shall spend some time on the concrete problems connected with establishing and developing this relationship.

The ambiguity of feelings

Whether confessional or secular, contemporary religious experiences affect human emotion: they are compelling, moving, and often at the root of an inner mood that lasts several days. Many pastors or pastoral ministers are surprised to see young and not-so-young people absorbed in their feelings; they even go so far as to criticize them severely, having the impression that their supposedly spiritual search is much more a search for a certain mood than a search for the living God. They think of certain Gospel passages: "Not everyone who says to me, 'Lord, Lord,' will enter the kingdom of heaven, but only the one who does the will of my Father in heaven" (Matt. 7:21). It seems to them that the basic duty of the Christian is to be engaged in accordance with the will of God and that this duty somehow prohibits the cultivation of spiritual experiences.

Indeed, it is a good thing to practise caution regarding the emotional aspect of our religious experience, for concentrating entirely on what is taking place within us when we pray or meditate can make an idol of our mood. We may end up absolutizing the world of feelings, wanting to take steps to ensure that they are always positive, constantly fostering our emotional state, "aestetize" our emotions—even the painful ones—enjoying them in an adolescent manner, and withdrawing into our own interiority. Falling into this attitude would entail the risk of bypassing all the good to be accomplished, the deep values that call out for our response, projects to be carried out, and people to love. The danger of just revelling in the world of feelings is real and it is important to be made aware of this. A critical distance is essential, for that is part of the Christian tradition.

Nevertheless, this same Christian tradition asks us to be open and sympathetic to spiritual seeking of an emotional nature. The wisdom of the spiritual doctrines has never demanded that purity and detachment be achieved overnight. It recognizes that feelings and entrancing experiences may be means the Holy Spirit uses to attract human beings to the Father. And, while it is a good idea to keep a certain distance with respect to spiritual phenomena, it is nonetheless necessary to unmask puritanical ways of handling transcendent experiences characterized by strong feelings. Such puritanism with respect to feelings devalues them and reduces faith to a question of meaning and commitment. All that would matter would be the meaning of life and engaged action. Would this not represent the old emphasis of modern times on reason and will, just expressed in a different way? This emphasis might also be reinforced by a legacy of anti-quietism and the fear of facing our own personal interiority.

Our feelings are ambiguous. Indeed, they may conceal from us the personal Presence offering itself to us at the heart of a spiritual experience. But may they not also serve as indicators of a reality that allows itself to be glimpsed as different from what we thought? Are we sufficiently aware of the help that our feelings give us in our discoveries and our re-discoveries of meaning? Really, our feelings are often bearers of perceptions that can bring us closer to God. They lead us to make spiritual breakthroughs and to become aware of intuitions whose existence we might otherwise never notice. If our feelings are prepared for and followed up by the quest for meaning, they will enable us to allow a Mystery to be born within us which concerns our entire being—mind, heart and soul.

In the transcendent experiences reported by phenomenologists and psychologists[10]—and these experiences are by no means limited to exceptional people—the associated feelings express a true openness of human consciousness to something that transcends it, to an indefinable reality appearing to be limitless. When these feelings are understood in relation to the deep desire of the human being, they become the vehicle that lets us come to the conviction that we have sensed a Reality capable of fulfilling our hope—perhaps a vague hope, but one that is always latent, nevertheless. Although the circumstances surrounding this key event may often be questionable, the perception that our nature is similar to that of the Source of all goodness and all value remains valid. "For we too are his offspring" (Acts 17:28). Amid intense feelings of peace, joy, or admiration, or even sadness, revulsion, or confusion, all human beings can welcome the visit of the unknown God whom they seek haphazardly and for whom their heart longs inescapably, despite all their disappointments and even their moments of resignation. They then need to follow their feelings all the way, right to the very depth of their being, where that love of God springs forth which alone can satisfy the heart. There is a danger, however, that while these feelings are indicative of a Presence, they may lose their transparency and thus turn the person inward instead of opening them up and bringing them into a conscious relationship with the One asking to be invited in. A force that is supposed to be centrifugal unfortunately then becomes centripetal; instead of being the medium that signals the possibility of an incomparable relationship, the feelings themselves take up all the space and become established as idols. That is how ambiguous feelings are: they are just as likely to lead an individual to cultivate an interiority that is turned in on itself as they are to help a person develop an existential relationship with their God.

We see this ambiguity in the Judeo-Christian experience. As this is not the place to examine that subject in depth, we shall limit ourselves to recalling the important place feelings held for people of faith in the Bible, in their discovery of God, and the primordial role given to the word of God in interpreting their emotional experience and orienting it towards transcendence. While it is clear that biblical figures encountered God through experiences characterized by a wide range of intense feelings, it is equally apparent that they constantly "came up against God's word," so to speak. This word of God did not simply emanate from their human thinking as a pure interpretative reflection of their experience. When The Lord spoke and confronted his people, he revealed himself to be like a parent who intervened in the evolution of his children by opposing certain directions their desire was taking them and by offering new paths for their desire. Our ancestors in the faith encountered in God an Other who had to be reckoned with. This meant that they had the good fortune of not being able to withdraw into their desire and into the feelings nourishing that desire. The word of God was for them like a principle of moral and spiritual reality that allowed them to utilize their feelings, that is to say, to be served by them rather than to serve them. The word of God invited them to go beyond their feelings to seek the moral reality emphasized by the Law as well as the spiritual reality which both permeated and transcended their lived experience.[11]

The purpose of these reflections is to show both the importance and the ambiguity that feelings hold for the Christian life. On the one hand, feelings open a person to the only One who can fulfill him or her; on the other hand, they can become obsessions and turn an individual or a religious group in on itself. The role of the word of God is to interpret and situate our experience of God which takes place through desire and feelings; it gives meaning and direction to the felt experience of a Reality which surpasses this experience itself; it opens the meditating or praying person to the imperatives of loving one's neighbour and searching for God.

Escape or embodiment?

Whether we are talking about a discovery made in prayer or in meditation, spiritual experience may just as easily lead to an escape from reality as to an embodiment of the religious intuitions gained, in the form of a more human lifestyle. It all depends on the overall attitude one is inclined to take towards existence. If the spiritual logic in question drives us to turn our back on ethical considerations, this logic would need to be liberated or even reversed. Therefore, a search for interiority aimed at escaping our personal problems, denying our finiteness or getting lost in a void sometimes called divine, can only be a rationalization for insensitivity to the needs of our neighbour, considered to be as illusory as our own. If, on the other hand, the spiritual dynamic moves the person to be more open to the demands of being human, the movement is a good one and its direction is in keeping with the Gospel.

The principle of embodiment plays a crucial role here. Jesus showed us that his prayer did not develop in isolation, but had a decisive in-fluence on the way he related to others. His intimacy with the Father allowed him to discern clearly and assume courageously his own mis-sion. His personal relationship with God, whose benevolent plan was to reign over humanity, impelled him to give his life to realize this reign of justice and love. That is why Jesus recognizes as worthy of the Kingdom only those for whom the service of others occupies a primary place: "Truly, I tell you, just as you did it to one of the least of these who are members of my family, you did it to me" (Matt. 25:40). The discovery of the God of Jesus can only make the believer more sensitive to the demands of justice; the encounter with God who became human can only encourage believers to embody in their relationships with others the love they experience in prayer.

If therefore spiritual experience is truly oriented in a realistic direction, it will impact on two important areas of human life: the psychological and the socio-political. In our culture, so affected by the human sciences and the mass media, spiritually oriented persons cannot exempt themselves from taking a stand with respect to what is being advocated by experts in humanist psychology and by groups dedicated to promoting various kinds of social causes. To think one could remain neutral here would amount to a dangerous illusion. Even the "pure contemplative" in our Christian tradition, the cloistered nun or monk, cannot abstain today from becoming informed about what is going on in the world and crying out for the coming of that reign of God to which Jesus gave himself entirely.[12]

The first area in which spiritual people must embody their experience of God is that of psychology. In the Thomist perspective, where grace does not destroy nature but rather perfects it, and where the virtuous humanization of the human being extends to all aspects of the personality, it is important to take seriously the invitation to grow psychologically. The reason for this is that, in order to activate the love received from God, believers need not only to have a conversion of heart, but also to use all their emotional resources: "You shall love the Lord your God with all your heart, and with all your soul, and with all your mind, and with all your strength... you shall love your neighbour as yourself" (Mark 12:30-31). Now, the wisdom and the methods of contemporary psychology can make a great contribution towards the elimination of obstacles that prevent us from loving with our whole being.

However, it is often the case that the ideals of material comfort and pleasure advocated by many psychologists turn spiritually inclined persons against the methods and practices of psychology. In several prayer groups, you will find a malaise or a disagreement between the goal of individual fulfillment and that of Christian transcendence. The result is a more or less openly stated distrust of the world of psychologists, psychiatrists, educators and social workers. People choose to see religious salvation and human therapies as being in opposition to one another. I think this opposition jeopardizes the ability to embody spiritual experience, which requires precisely a coming to terms with our personal problems so that the grace of salvation may penetrate every fibre of our being. Instead of turning their backs on psychology, men and women of prayer should be bold enough to utilize the contributions it can make while at the same time rectifying its basic orientations where necessary. For example, they could emphasize that the meaning of life does not consist of becoming wrapped up in the worship of the ego but in developing oneself as a human being in order to be able to make one's contribution to the reign of God. With this re-orientation of its basic premise, psychology can be of great service in bringing to concrete expression that which is discovered in spiritual experience and in enabling believers to let that discovery enter into their whole being.

The same challenge is addressed to spiritual people by the socio-political forces that shape the way we live collectively. Women and men who are spiritually inclined are frequently intimidated by the complexity of social organization and fear they will be tricked by those who propose, sometimes quite aggressively, solutions that appear dogmatic and simplistic. To avoid "moral contamination," they refuse to work with people who do not share their faith; to safeguard their serenity and their inner mood, they are inclined to remain inactive and to turn a deaf ear to the calls of those who want them to share their social and political views; finally, a certain weariness and veiled scepticism with respect to the future of society drives them to withdraw into their spiritual enthusiasm and their cozy fellowship, where they hope that the transforming of hearts will automatically lead to social renewal.

Since we need to clarify here what the conditions are for a spiritual experience to be open to the whole of reality, it must be said that the two forms of spiritualism that we have just described cannot claim to be in keeping with the Gospel. They in fact impede the embodiment of love either in the human psyche or in the mediation of society. By lapsing into them, we stop taking seriously the ethical dimension of our lives. By circumscribing God within some sacred territory and not letting God penetrate the dark parts of either our personality or our social structures, we close ourselves off from the emotional and historical requirements of salvation, we maintain a breach between dimensions of human life which, in biblical people of faith and in Jesus, existed in dynamic relationship. Indeed, for spiritual experience to be fully human, it must foster self-knowledge and action.

Please understand what I mean by these remarks. I am not trying to admonish people for a lack of attention to their psychological reality or a lack of participation in social struggle. What is required is not so much to be extremely advanced with respect to emotional balance and engaged action, but rather to seek to improve oneself in both of these areas and to realize that this progress is part of Christian liberation of the whole person. That is why it is important for pastoral caregivers to distinguish clearly between spiritual experience that opens people up to a better relationship with themselves and with others and spiritual experience that cuts people off from reality by fostering escape into an artificial interiority.

From short-lived to lasting

In this era of instant coffee, TV dinners and "solid state" appliances that don't even need a few seconds to warm up but play as soon as the button is pressed, we are accustomed to getting results easily and immediately. Many people expect the same thing when it comes to spiritual matters; they imagine that within a few weeks or even days, they can become proficient at meditating, become a man or woman of prayer, a psychologically liberated human being or a devoted follower of Jesus Christ. It is sad to see that there are pseudo-experts in human relations or spirituality today who, out of greed or the desire for success and influence, exploit the trust of such people seeking wisdom and happiness. By contrast, the true spiritual master, whether guru, psychologist or shaman, never pretends that the inner journey will be easy or short. They will certainly admit the value of a spiritual breakthrough, a conversion or a new horizon suddenly becoming manifest; but they know that such a phenomenon has had a long preparation and must be followed up by a long struggle. That is why they will readily compare religious growth to life and to the maturing of an organism whose development depends on several factors, which are themselves subject to time. For religious growth to be lasting, the following factors must play a part: ethical detachment, the reference group, spiritual techniques and the sense of gift.

The spiritual life does not function independently of the ethical life. Therefore, it normally exercises influence over a person's lifestyle, engendering a certain serenity and re-ordering of priorities. But when no limit is imposed upon it, the spiritual life goes much farther: on the one hand, it strongly connects the believer to deep values and encourages the investment of all one's energies into promoting them; on the other, it not only detaches the believer from anti-values but also from the individualistic pursuit of self-actualization. This latter form of detachment is particularly difficult to achieve in a Western culture, which insists a great deal on the development of the personality. This emphasis is so great that, when inviting people to become engaged in a spiritual experience, it is quite natural to have to point out to them what personal advantage they will gain from it. While it may be inevitable to have to start off that way in order to encourage beginners, the fact remains that authentic spiritual conversion leads the initiated to entrust their development to God and to follow wholeheartedly what he desires for them and for those around them.

The second factor in lasting religious growth deals with the communal aspect of religious experience. At the start of the journey, one looks for mutual support to a reference group where one somehow feels the presence of God through shared fervour. Then, the connection that exists among the members of the group deepens, insofar as they are interested in things that go beyond just the benefits of prayer or meditation, insofar as they deepen their commitment to a common destiny they are called to live, insofar as they are passionately concerned about carrying out the will of God in their own lives and in the world. Such a community becomes all the stronger when it reaches outward and intensifies its desire to be a partner in God's plan through love. This solidarity allows it to get through tough times and to shoulder the weaknesses of its members. When the community perceives God as infinitely greater than itself, it becomes an energizing space where each member's joy consists in giving their life so that God may be better known and loved.

The attitude towards methods for developing interiority constitutes a third factor determining lasting religious growth. The person of prayer or who meditates is not above the use of techniques; he or she will appreciate the precariousness of their fidelity sufficiently to see the wisdom of such recourse and will, moreover, know how to adapt such techniques to their own temperament and rhythm. Without diminishing the value of method—which through God's grace humans may use to advantage—the prayerful person nevertheless gives priority to motives. At the start of the journey, the attraction of exploring the self, the desire for religious feelings, and the satisfaction of attaining a healing unity and balance, all play a more important role. But spiritual progress soon halts if the motive is not transformed into a willingness to love God for his own sake. The techniques and methods that produced good results become merely relative as one increasingly discovers how much the reality of God transcends the medium used and how much God's presence is offered as a free gift.

Finally, the fourth factor in lasting spiritual experience is the sense of gift. Once we have understood that the spiritual life is not a matter of human conquest, but rather is something given by God, we no longer rely on our own strength but on grace. We then become less susceptible to discouragement, knowing in whom we have placed our trust. The climate of inner experience then consists of peace and thanksgiving. It is also easier to acknowledge one's weaknesses and even to learn to make use of them. Any feelings of self-sufficiency or superiority having been thoroughly eroded, we become humbler towards others, more able to share and be in mutual solidarity with them. And in the time of trial, which always follows on the heels of progress in prayer, one remains calm in the face of the turmoil of temptation, the lucid perception of one's lack of love, and the impossible vision of God.

Given the numerous forms of spiritual experience that people have today, we recognize that authenticity is possible in all who are open to establishing and developing a relationship with a transcendent Reality. With maximum confidence in the various Christian and non-Christian movements appearing today, we have singled out three major problems concerning this existential relationship with the One towards whom religious experience normally opens us. Firstly, the feelings may either turn the person in on herself or help her strengthen her faith in the One who is Life and Love. Secondly, spiritual experience can either remain isolated from the rest of existence or it can be embodied in enriched personal emotions coupled with a more resolute commitment to others. Thirdly, interiority will have the best chance of remaining a lasting dimension if the individual consents to ethical detachment, communal solidarity, moderate use of techniques and an absolute trust in the gift of God.

With respect to each of these problems, one who witnesses to Jesus can play an important role. Inspired by the word of God and its rich spiritual tradition, that person can accompany non-Christians and Christians alike on their journey and deal with any sincere quest for wisdom. To do this, he or she must not demand that the quest be immediately transplanted into the soil of the Gospel. Today many people, in fact, seek God without naming him, and they need help in confirming and correcting their path. If we want to give them this help, we need to put ourselves in their place and discern with them what comes from the evil spirit and what comes from the Holy Spirit. It seems to me that presenting criteria that can be applied equally well in non-confessional and in Christian contexts can help witnesses to the Gospel situate themselves and be in active solidarity with today's spiritual renewal.

10

The Gospel and Everyday Life

It used to be common, and sometimes still is, to speak of a discon-
nection between liturgy and life. How many people complained
they saw no relationship between Sunday Mass and the events of
the week, until one day, like so many others, they quit going and joined
the growing numbers of non-practising Catholics! The liturgy did not
help them in the least to see a link between the Christian mystery and
their family context, their work environment, and the social fabric
they were part of. Even now, do the words used in our celebrations
really refer, in any meaningful way, to our daily life in the home or at
school, in the office or at the hospital, at the store or at the plant? Do
they address the importance of our collective existence? Above all,
do the words spoken at our Christian gatherings give meaning to the
events and situations that touch us and that we spend time wondering
about?

Liturgy and human experience, for the longest time, constituted
two separate, even watertight, compartments. This phenomenon
should not have surprised us, for we knew we had inherited a liturgy
that was adapted to a culture of the distant past. Only when the texts
of the Mass were translated into the vernacular did it become blatantly
clear just how ill-adapted that liturgy was to our contemporary world.
Eventually we were forced to accept the huge challenge of adapting
a liturgy that was behind in terms of our mindsets and our sensibilities. Fortunately, this process of transformation is now established as
ongoing, with respect to both the spoken word and other modes of
expression.

I will confine myself here to issues that concern the words spoken by the presider, particularly, in the homily. However, I am keen
to point out that it is equally essential to adapt that other aspect of
language that consists of religious expression through the symbolism

of images, objects, gestures and actions. Moreover, I believe that if we have thoroughly grasped the challenge of adapting the spoken word in such a way as to give meaning to a celebration, then we will be well poised to modify existing rituals or create new ones in a way that remains in complete fidelity to the mystery made present in the sacrament.

To successfully adapt our speech is to speak in a manner that lets us be understood. Two approaches that have been advocated for many years achieve this goal. I will begin by reviewing these two forms of adaptation, before suggesting another method that should help to restore the connection between the mystery being celebrated in the Eucharist and the everyday lives of those doing the celebrating.

The texts as the starting point

For several decades now, we have been witnessing two kinds of efforts at adapting liturgical communication. The first might be compared to a downward movement, going from the liturgical texts to everyday life, while the second is like an upward movement, going from everyday life to the religious reality being celebrated. Unfortunately these two movements have not produced all the hoped-for results, in the one case, because it limited itself to a kind of exegesis, and in the other, because it often simply presented life in moral, psychological, or sociological categories. Let us examine in greater detail these two approaches and see what is preventing them from being really effective.

The first way of bringing liturgy and life closer together consists of trying to help people access the Scriptures. As people already had some familiarity with this movement, it became fairly common after Vatican II, when the sermon was replaced by the homily. Influenced by the renewal in biblical studies and aware of the incomparable value of the word of God, homilists strove to explain the various readings proclaimed during the liturgy of the Word. They tried to make the old biblical vocabulary more comprehensible by using words that were more familiar to their listeners. Their efforts were exegetical as well as catechetical; it was a matter of clarifying terms by situating them in their original context, relating them to the whole of Christian belief, and showing their relevance through some applications to life. The weakness of this clarification was that it offered an understanding of

Scripture that did not necessarily relate to people's daily concerns. When homilies stick to explanations, they may stimulate cognitive interest, but do they help listeners find concrete meaning in their everyday experience?

Many priests see the homily as a teaching opportunity. They tell themselves, "The people don't understand the texts that are read or the symbolic gestures made in the liturgy. So, I'm going to explain them." Thus, the homily and other interventions by the presider get transformed into occasions for mini-catechesis. While not denying that these doctrinal clarifications have some value, I believe that the liturgy of the Word must have a different purpose: conveying vital meaning. To really bring out the meaning of everyday life experience for listeners, through the help of the word of God, requires more than just giving information and explanations. To suggest an existential response that fits with the experience of our contemporaries requires more than just presenting principles, ideas or reflections.

We might ask ourselves whether this doctrinal orientation is what accounts for the lack of pertinence of much of what is said in our churches. The language used in the liturgy does not get the message across. Whether their source is biblical or contemporary, the key words of our religious vocabulary do not convey what they are supposed to. Kingdom, heaven, hell, immortality, resurrection, charity, grace, sin, judgment, and so on—these terms suggest something totally different than what they should be guiding us towards! We can no longer use them with the assumption that they will be properly understood, for that would be to lead people down the wrong path and to fall into old ways devoid of the real sap of the Gospel. In our efforts to reform our language, we learn to distrust words. Even if they have content, they are not necessarily meaning-filled, for they may not evoke any experience the person in the pew can relate to. For example, what meaning can the image of God as king, all-powerful monarch, or sovereign judge hold for people today? Does this type of representation not risk leading us towards a different God than the Father of Jesus? If we want to avoid leading people into error, will it be enough to use synonyms for words that are hard to extricate from a culture whose points of reference we do not share? To take another example, does not even the image of God the Father risk provoking a mixed reaction—often unexpressed—in people who wonder who they really believe in? If, with even a minimum of psychological information, we are no longer able to believe that the experience of father, in our world today, is necessarily a positive one, must we not conclude that the meaning of this expression is no longer obvious?

In the face of traditional kinds of language, which have lost their transparency for our contemporaries, we need to recognize that our efforts at exegesis and explanation finally amount to wasting our breath. Many pastors who are sufficiently in tune with the ascendant culture to note the opaqueness of traditional religious vocabulary, have, on seeing this, been moved to take a different tack, to start from below, that is from the concrete, to go from there to the word of God.

Life as the starting point

While the first adaptation movement tries to explain the traditional language of religious truths, the second movement, which I would call the upward movement, starts with life, trying to move from there to the revealed text and to the reality being celebrated. A question is raised, an event is recounted, a situation is presented that the listeners can understand without difficulty. This way of proceeding aims to relate daily life to the Christian mystery: I find it excellent insofar as this relationship is achieved. To do so, it is necessary to go beyond the point of departure. A student said to me once, "The priest at our parish always has good lead-ins to his homilies: he refers to things really happening today. But he doesn't know how to follow through. He whets our appetite and then leaves us hanging." Like many of us, this priest sets out from the concrete, but then only skims the surface of everyday life. It is not enough to describe and mirror real life experience; one must go further and discern its religious significance.

Unfortunately, this religious significance is frequently expressed in moral terms. We talk to people about the things that make up their life, but concentrate on the ethical requirements of the Gospel when showing its application. Just prior to the recitation of the Our Father, for example, a presider might remind the congregation that it is not enough to recite these petitions, but that we must put them into practice. Good moral teaching but totally out of context! In the celebration as a whole, the ethical dimension needs to remain secondary to that of meaning. I don't think people come to church just to have someone tell them, "Take time for others, respect your neighbour, help them out," but rather something like, "By freely following the love he had within him through to the end, Jesus teaches us the secret of existence, which consists of caring for others, respecting them, and helping them; and by raising him from the dead, the Father assures us that this is the path that leads to life." Grasping the meaning of life can sharpen our grasp of ethical demands, but the problem of values only makes us ask the question of religious meaning. What is expected of Christians, especially those gathered for liturgy, is to be able to proclaim a hope that gives meaning to life, not to proclaim a moral wisdom, no matter how good.

Another way we get stuck at the moral level is by applying any reading of the signs of the times to the identification of values. This approach fails to draw from the signs of the times everything they can tell us. Why would we care that a particular problem or event indicates that a particular value is at stake, if we have not been touched in our respective aspirations or longings and if we fail to see how Jesus can satisfy them? A good interpretation, then, of the signs of the times should be able to cut across any ethical concerns and discern what needs to be liberated. It should recognize in the groaning of the Spirit the expression of human concerns.

A reading of life that is purely moral—even in the loftiest sense of the term—is perhaps the greatest obstacle, precisely because of its loftiness, to a deeper adaptation of the liturgy. When liturgical language keeps our attention focused at the level of ethical demands such as guiding others to find fulfillment, building the human community, or building social solidarity, it remains immersed in psychology and sociology, playing a strictly functional role, one of moral sensitization. By not leaving the practical realm, it serves a different purpose from what it is intended for. The true role of liturgical language is rather, while expressing ethical demands, to refer us back to Jesus, who is present at the heart of these demands, so that we may enter into a mystery that contextualizes and enlivens these demands and at the same time transcends them. In short, a moralizing liturgy, even within a movement of renewal, can never be a meaningful celebration of our deep human experience.

The nature of the challenge

The two kinds of adaptation I have just described, while they are searching in the right direction, share the weakness of remaining unable to identify the true connection that exists between the Christian mystery and human experience. We have seen that it does not suffice to explain the language of the past or to apply the Gospel to situations where moral values come into play. The challenge we must take up is rather to bring to light the Gospel meaning of our life, to be able to perceive in our human experience the reality being celebrated. What is it, then, that we are celebrating in the liturgy? The death and resurrection of Jesus and our own, we answer. But do we have any experience of this death and resurrection? Are we capable of recognizing Christian liberation when it takes place? Is the Christian liberation that we celebrate sacramentally recognizable in one form or another in our daily lives?

I think it is. I think it is possible for us to identify, in our human experience, the desire to be liberated and also to identify the partial fulfillment of that desire. And I will add that if we cannot do that, then we hardly know what we are celebrating; if the sacrament does not relate to anything we can identify in our lives, it cannot hold any meaning for us whatsoever, it cannot be a sign of a greater and fuller reality. Thus, we are faced with the necessity of finding in our concrete existence traces of the paschal mystery of Jesus, but we must admit that a certain "supernaturalism" did not prepare us in any way for deciphering the Gospel as embodied in our everyday lives.

To help us discern the paschal mystery at work in our daily life, I would like to describe now a practical method that comprises two stages. We will begin by casting a first glance at some aspect of our human experience to reflect on what is happening there and how it is being experienced. After that, we will be in a position to re-visit this same aspect, taking a second look at it, and grasping its Christian meaning.

A first glance

At this first stage, we try to think of an event, a situation, a slice of life that holds importance for whomever we are addressing. It could be any experience whatsoever, as long as there really is something of human value at stake in it. We need to evoke the feelings and the questions involved in that experience. To carry this out two attitudes are required. First, there needs to be empathy: we must be active and understanding listeners in order to be able to re-express lived experience in a way that can reach a group of people. Secondly, we must be able to let the real questions concerning human existence emerge and to know how to address them.

The first attitude—tuning in to those in one's milieu – is only possible if one journeys with them and shares in their experiences, their good times and bad, their hopes and their sorrows. This attitude demands paying close attention to what they say as well as what they do not say. It demands not projecting one's personal needs onto them, but rather observing, consulting, and remaining constantly attentive to reactions, before claiming to know the exact context or climate in which people experience their interests and concerns, their worries and their sufferings. The second attitude presupposes great intellectual integrity: it consists of letting life's great questions come to the fore, not seeking refuge in ready-made answers, and keeping open in one's mind an area of uncertainty and searching. One must maintain attitudes of permissiveness and confidence in the intelligence of others, as these attitudes will foster their quest for meaning and their finding explanations. In summary, two inseparable skills are required: the empathy to be able to welcome, as expressed through their feelings, a lived experience packed with problems, observations, and desires; and the wisdom to welcome the questions, the intuitions, and the fragmented truths that people carry within them.

Thus, in the first stage, adaptation to lived experience consists of reflecting on it in a way that brings out what is important, meaningful and pertinent. In other words, we must manage to express in the liturgy both the religious experience and the quest for meaning of people today. Religious experience includes any human experience sufficiently dense to have a window on a transcendent dimension of reality. The quest for meaning is a search which is not satisfied by immediate meaning, but which demands, through all the intermediate levels, a comprehensive meaning that is the foundation for all the others and makes hope in life possible. Christian gatherings must evoke one or another of the myriad forms of religious experience that reveal the openness of human emotion to transcendence, that betray the yearning of the human heart for something beautiful, something great, something comforting. Interpersonal relations, the great moments in life, the seasons, nature, art: these are but a few examples of places where religious experience is possible. These are also opportunities to ponder the meaning of existence, which show the human being's insatiable desire to understand. These numerous opportunities allow us to cast a first glance at the many forms our life experience takes.

A second look

By not skipping that first glance at human experience, we will be better equipped to take a second look that is not artificial, imaginary or foreign. To the extent that our first glance deals with an experience opening onto a dimension or meaning which both assumes and transcends that experience, the second look, that of faith and the interpretation of life, will be taken in continuity with the first, illuminating it, deepening it, and conferring on it its supernatural significance. From everyday life to the Gospel and from the Gospel to everyday life, the shift will be quite a natural one. Indeed, our first glance at a situation or a slice of life offers the word of God raw material that has already been pre-interpreted and is open to comprehensive meaning. How many facts of our existence thus constitute the raw material for the parables of the Kingdom! Conversely, this or that passage of the Gospel will allow us to discover a wealth of things about our own lived experience and the lived experience of those around us.

In other words, the language of an adapted liturgy requires constant mediation between human experience and the mystery being celebrated. I am struck by how much, in certain Gospel sharings, very concrete readings of experience are able to enrich the understanding of the Jesus event and, how much, in turn, the word of the Gospel brings out the meaning hidden in our experience. The language of the faithful gathered together allows countless links to be established between human experience and the word of God, and a series of signs to be discerned that manifest Christian liberation at work in individuals and in society. This process of revisiting our experience, carried out in the light of the revealed word, constitutes an understandable way of approaching the Good News as well as an invitation to convert to it. Moreover, the second look, taken in a community of faith, is not limited to mirroring and expressing lived experience; it can resolve any discord between our own paths and the path of God exemplified in Jesus; the second look exercises, here and now, the prophetic role of revealing the drama of our inhumanity and of denouncing our passivity and our despair. It is only when Christian language goes to the trouble of becoming meaningful that the liturgy becomes the place where the message of the Spirit can be offered for existential acceptance. For no proposal can be either accepted or rejected unless we find in it some relevance in relation to ourselves.

An example

We could illustrate in a thousand and one ways this manner of building bridges between life and the mystery we celebrate in the liturgy. For example, here is the kind of interpretation that was suggested in a homily at the time of the Montreal Olympic Games. The homilist began by noting the deep divisions and the difficult tensions that had marked the education and hospital sectors in the spring of 1976. Then he cited the second reading for that Sunday, Ephesians 2:13-18, where the writer speaks of the wall of incomprehension, even hatred, dividing social classes and peoples, noting how fear and ambition (especially economic) tend to cause both material and psychological barriers that separate people.

That was, however, only one side of the coin. In addition to abundant data showing how we are continually trying to bridge the gaps that isolate us from one another, the particular event of the Olympics revealed that our desire for peace can and often does go even further. Looking past the regrets many people had about excessive expenses, others felt that these games expressed an admiration, shared by all nations, for the energy and agility of the human body and that, by bringing together representatives from so many countries, the games became a symbol of universal peace, friendship and kinship. As these values are hardly practised in reality, the question arose whether this was the celebration of a utopia. Then, the resurrection of Jesus was presented as the great sign that the good news of peace was not illusory, but that it had begun to be realized. After having enabled us for

2000 years to interpret the great aspirations and modest realizations of Christians, the Gospel would no doubt be able to help us celebrate the Olympics in the broader perspective of our faith and our hope.

Two problems

We might object that events like the Olympics are not going to arise every week and that it is hard for a parish priest to find meaningful events or situations. This objection prompts me to question the fact that a liturgy can be prepared and carried out by just one man. A thorough adaptation of a liturgy requires a range of skills that a single individual will not easily possess. On the other hand, when liturgy teams bring together people of varied backgrounds and walks of life to take responsibility for adapting the celebrations to personal, family, and collective experience, the chances of getting it right increase tremendously.

A second problem relates to the fact that, quite often, the members of a parish hardly know one another and have no common experience that the liturgical presider can rely on or refer to in his efforts to speak in a way that will connect life and the mystery being celebrated. I think that the beginnings of a solution can be found in personalizing the Sunday celebrations. Already, in certain parishes, the Saturday evening Mass has a different character from the first one on Sunday morning, and it differs again from the last morning Mass. It seems to me that short of turning into spiritual gas stations, churches can no longer keep gathering together anyone and everyone anytime. It would be highly desirable, on the contrary, if every regular Eucharistic gathering could take on its own unique characteristics and orientation and if its participants remained faithful to that particular gathering. Meeting on a regular basis, talking to one another, sharing concerns and even common projects can only bring parish community members gradually closer. It might happen that, as a consequence, people will want to live their Christian solidarity even more fully and choose to celebrate at such a gathering not only the Eucharist, but also other sacraments such as Baptism and funeral rites.

While the homily is the place par excellence for highlighting the relationship between the paschal mystery and the everyday lives of the faithful, it is still true that there remain other parts of the liturgy, like the opening instruction, the penitential preparation, the presider's prayers and the universal prayer, which provide the celebrants and the congregation with many opportunities to add spoken words that help make the connection with human life. In each of these speaking instances, we face the difficulty of bringing to light the real meaning of our lived experience and of the celebration, while ensuring that text explanations and moral exhortations remain secondary. The practical method which consists of doing two successive takes on a human situation can help us meet the challenge of interpreting events concretely in the light of the word of God, provided we agree to personalize liturgical language in accordance with the milieu in which we live.

Part IV

CRITICAL DIALOGUE

11

On Reincarnation

Jean-Luc Hétu makes the case that Christians should be open to reincarnation in his book *Réincarnation et foi chrétienne.*[13] Writing as a thinker who is completely free with respect to religious traditions, Hétu interprets reincarnation as well as Christian faith. His work is relevant because his reflections address concerns that are on the minds of many in the Western world today. But it is problematic because it distorts not only belief in reincarnation but also the elements of Christianity that he retains: they are removed from the contexts that give them meaning. Hétu fails to make clear the enormous difference that exists between Eastern and Western attitudes to reincarnation. For a Hindu or a Buddhist, reincarnation is an unhappy and dreaded fate; for an optimist like Hétu, who believes in the evolution of humanity and the psychological growth of individuals, reincarnation becomes simply the opportunity for human progress, which he considers inevitable in the long term,[14] I question whether it is possible for Christianity to accept reincarnation, whether understood in the Eastern or in the Western sense, without denying several of its own basic convictions. I would like to draw attention to three of these basic convictions and discuss briefly the issues that emerge. We will look at salvation, grace, and our notion of God; individual personality; and access to truth.

1. Salvation, grace and our notion of God

In Chapter 3 of his book, Hétu rightly rejects a salvation gained and granted by Christ in such a way that it would miraculously take care of all a person's problems. Understanding salvation in this way produces a false sense of security and casts doubt on the reality of salvation, given that there would be plenty of evidence to show that the person's problems were in fact not resolved at all. When Hétu talks about personal problems and personal growth, it seems to me that he is dealing with the psychological and moral level. In that regard, he sheds a certain light on human existence. We must not forget that, generally speaking, the Christianity that we have inherited was almost completely lacking in the psychological dimension of salvation and its moral dimension was often reduced to a legalistic perspective.

For his part, unfortunately, Hétu fails to appreciate another dimension of salvation, namely the religious dimension: humanity's relationship with the living God. Hétu's book takes this relationship for granted, but in a vague manner that is not very interpersonal. "God" does not seem to be a Presence that amazes, disturbs, and fascinates, but rather a condition of possibility for human development. Thus—and this is but one example among others—Hétu does not speak of resurrection as an unprecedented encounter between humans and God, in which God gifts us with the divine life of love and fullness. Here is an example of how this great reality is downgraded in Hétu's work:

> Following the logic of what has been said thus far, to believe in the resurrection of the dead, to believe in my resurrection, is to believe in the mysterious permanence, by the grace of God, of all that I have learned as a human being, which has been gradually entered into my personal story, and also to believe in the mysterious permanence of all my positive interventions, which have been entered into the whole of history, in solidarity with others. (pp. 61–62) [translation]

A careful reading of chapter 3 and of pages 68 to 71 of chapter 5 is sufficient to realize that Hétu's interpretation of grace reduces it to a gift from God in the order of creation, a gift from God operating in the framework of the natural activities of the human being. I am delighted that Hétu shows us this dimension, but I deplore this reduction of grace, which must be seen in relation to his failure to appreciate the specifically religious aspect of the Christian life. If history were seen as a love story between God and humanity, in which the latter, free to accept God's love, rejected it and went off the tracks—religiously, morally and psychologically—and if we truly believed that God, in his goodness, renewed the offer of his love to humanity through a concrete gesture of forgiveness, made visible in Jesus Christ, then how would it be possible to circumvent this relational character of salvation and deal only, for all practical purposes, with its psychological and moral dimension?

Emptying Christianity of its central mystery as he does, Hétu is nevertheless able to establish interesting similarities between different traditions. However, he forgets that reincarnation is a belief generally held by people for whom God is not a personal Presence who creates and forgives freely, whose grace indeed "solves" the deepest human problem, and whose offer of attention and friendship to believers has the power to draw them out of their fundamental loneliness.

2. Individual personality

As God is not, for Hétu, a living God capable of freely giving his friendship anew to human beings, a God who in so doing becomes their radical salvation, it is not in the least surprising that the idea of definitive forgiveness, which goes beyond simple human maturing, has hardly any meaning for him. On page 12 of *Réincarnation et foi chrétienne*, he does say that "the reincarnationist point of view makes possible a harmonious synthesis of God's justice and mercy" [translation]. When we look at this closely, however, we note that Hétu's definition of mercy brings it within the bounds of justice: he sees mercy as the opportunity we would be given to start another existence as long as our human learning had not been completed. Let us also note that human freedom is not taken seriously enough, for, in this optimistic vision, no one can give God a final no: "God's plan is in effect to bring to completion every process of spiritual maturing undertaken by each of his creatures" (p. 13) [translation]. The human odyssey thus becomes a trajectory with safe arrival always guaranteed no matter what mistakes are made en route. This absence of real freedom, of a freedom capable of accepting or rejecting God's offer of forgiveness, is Hétu's first contravention of individual personality.

Hétu's second contravention concerns the relationship between personality and corporeality. Even though many Christians have been influenced by one form or another of body/soul dualism, Christianity holds the conviction that the human body and soul are substantially one. People should, in fact, be able to say of themselves, "I am this soul incorporated in this body," or, if you like, "I am this body animated by this soul." In the context of this anthropology, which is both biblical and personalist, the resurrection is to be seen not as the resuscitation of specific matter, but as the whole person—body and soul—receiving a life of fullness rooted in God's presence to humanity and the cosmos. Even if we accept a healthy agnosticism—based on 1 Cor. 15—with respect to the modalities of the resurrection, we can nevertheless get a faint idea based on a philosophy of the body as expression of our interiority, and as our way of communicating with others and with the universe. The resurrection consists, then, in a deep renewal of persons and of their ability to express themselves and communicate, while respecting individual identities.

This respect for individual identities would not be maintained if there were successive reincarnations. In fact, the human body is more than a biological reality: it is the tangible aspect of a personality, with characteristic manners and attitudes, a culture, a language, a memory, and a particular way of entering into relationship with others. How could an individual who lived in Quebec in the twentieth century remain the same, reincarnated in China in the twenty-first century? How could she not help but become a totally other person, having received an entirely different set of genes from new parents and receiving, in the early years, a completely different upbringing? I direct these questions to a Western psychologist like Hétu as I suspect that they would be meaningless in a Hindu perspective, where it is not the personality that is reincarnated, but a kind of psychic-spiritual energy. In contrast to Hétu, I maintain that the Hindu and Christian approaches to salvation are incompatible and that even the approaches of Hinduism and North American psychology are incompatible. Indeed, for Hindus, liberation consists of shedding the illusion of individual personality and losing oneself in a great divine all. On the contrary, for Christians—and for many psychologists—liberation consists not of abolishing the individual personality, but of each person opening up to God and to others. It is not a matter of fusion with God but of a union, which, in the words of Teilhard de Chardin, differentiates.

Hétu's work does contain passages that make an intelligent comparison between reincarnation and purgatory. I agree with his criticism of Küng's position, according to which the believer is brought to perfection immediately upon death, with no need of a period of time to integrate God's love into every aspect of her being (see pp. 150-155). Of course, purgatory must be demythologized and situated within the more central mystery of the resurrection. In this regard, I personally deplore how numerous biblical scholars dismiss out of hand the doctrine of purgatory without exploring sufficiently the renewed meaning that may be found in it. (K. Rahner and R. Ombres are guides who can help us rediscover this meaning for today.) Hétu has seen clearly the role that purgatory can play within the larger context of Christian beliefs. Roughly speaking, purgatory and reincarnation address similar concerns. The advantage purgatory has over reincarnation is that once thought through in terms of the overall perspective of the Christian mystery, purgatory can be integrated into the vision of the human as an inseparable unity of body and soul.

3. Access to truth

A third basic conviction taught by Christianity concerns access to truth. I find this basic conviction difficult to express, however, in a post-Christian society where the majority of people oscillate between dogmatism (less common than formerly with regard to religion, but now common in many other realms) and relativism. In the face of this tension, Hétu adopts—without identifying it as such—the relativist position. In the vocabulary he uses (see pp. 201–203), he rejects the "sectarian" (or dogmatic) attitude in favor of the "gnostic" (or relativist) attitude. In my view, the gnostic attitude he advocates is relativist in that beliefs are considered to be valid *relative to* the meaning they give to human experience. In this context, the question of the criteria for truth is hardly asked, despite a number of remarks Hétu makes which could have led him to raise this question explicitly (see, for example, p. 49).

I agree with Hétu about being open to the beliefs of others. Unfortunately, I am not certain that he himself is truly open to the wisdom offered by Eastern religions, since he accepts unquestioningly the way that theosophists or Western spiritual teachers have distorted reincarnation by inserting it into an evolutionist and/or psychological context. Whether Hétu is open or not, he is right to stress the importance of taking seriously the concerns of others which prompt them to accept a doctrine or to accept the meaning a doctrine has for their lives. People can encounter each other as they share these concerns and this search for meaning.

As the dialogue deepens, however, one is faced with a fundamental issue: one comes up against the difference between the level of concerns and meaning, on the one hand, and the level of truth, on the other. Whether dealing with reincarnation or any other subject, an idea may address concerns and offer meaning for many people without necessarily being true. To take an extreme example, Hitler's ideas regarding the mission and politics of the German nation met the concerns and the search for meaning of a people humiliated by their 1918 defeat and the ensuing fragile economy, yet his ideas were false. What I am trying to say is that the idea of reincarnation is an interesting idea, but raises problems that force us to doubt its truth. Having indicated some of these problems above, my conclusion is that, contrary to what Hétu maintains, reincarnation cannot be integrated into Christianity without Christianity becoming inconsistent with itself.

What Hétu seems to be unaware of is that the coherence of a comprehensive interpretation affects those who subscribe to it in such a way that they may see things very differently from those who are influenced by another coherent system. Contrary to what he writes, this holds equally true for therapists and practitioners in the human sciences. The more one studies a particular coherent system in depth, the more one becomes particular at the end of the process. Even if certain concerns are found to be analogous, the basic truths and the orientation of the practices will often prove to be irreconcilable. Recall what was said earlier about salvation, grace, our notion of God, forgiveness, the human personality, and access to truth. The more Hindus merge with the great all, the more they let go of their individuality (if indeed they believed they possessed an individuality). The closer Christians become to God, the more they affirm the otherness of God and his grace. The difference in perspective between the two is such that an authentic Hindu will no doubt feel uncomfortable with our Western manner of talking about this difference. And what about the myriad nuances in Hinduism? There are several streams within it to which my comments here will hardly apply.

The conclusion of *Réincarnation et foi chrétienne* confirms Hétu's relativist approach, since he retains, as a simple hypothesis, an idea that speaks to him and inspires him, namely, reincarnation. His work reflects the fragmentation of contemporary society, where a great variety of ideas is offered to everyone and large numbers of people find it impossible to assume their religious heritage in a critical manner. In the current climate, it is easy to be unaware of the problem of Christian identity. I do not deny the right of a thinker to reflect on what meaning the Christian faith might have in our culture. After all, that is what I too, like so many others for 2000 years, have been trying to do. What I take exception to is the manner of reinterpretation, which is not sensitive enough to the criteria for the coherence and truth of Christianity.

12

The Words of a Spiritual Master

As I am convinced that Karlfried Graf Dürckheim is a true spiritual master for our time, a time when spirituality and agnosticism are not seen as incompatible, I would like to offer some theological reflections on two of his books: *Our Twofold Origin* and *Dialogue on the Path of Initiation*.[15] I have read and reread these books and will provide numerous references to encourage the reader to go to the texts themselves, as these are very rich indeed.

The experience of Being

Born in 1896, Dürckheim received his psychological training in Germany in the 1920s; this meant his training had a conceptualist orientation. In 1937, he discovered Zen Buddhism in Japan. He expanded his knowledge by becoming an initiate. His theme of the two aspects of the human being is rooted in that experience. There is the Western side and the Eastern side, "the outer person" and "the inner person" (*Twofold*, 188), which need to be intimately united. There is the theme of the human's "double origin, in the earth and in the sky, in the natural and in the supernatural" (*Twofold*, 9). These two levels of human experience are in no way separate from one another: Dürckheim shows how we pass from the first—the pragmatic daily round, to the second—openness to transcendence. Furthermore, he shows how a good moral and psychological foundation is essential if people are to embody their religious intuitions in a fruitful manner. He sees the relationship between the two levels as complementary, and the way he deals with the limits of our natural consciousness (including meditation undertaken for non-religious reasons), on the one hand, and the dangers encountered by our supernatural consciousness, on the other, displays clearly his vast experience and deep wisdom. He believes in psychotherapy as much as in religious initiation (*Twofold*,

172), in the balance of the "natural man" as much as in the maturity of the "initiated man." He is demanding when he speaks of fidelity to one's Essential Being and of the steps that must be taken to maintain that fidelity. For him, a fresh effort is required daily if we are serious about listening to God; however, this discipline remains secondary to the role of illumination and grace (*Twofold*, ch. 5: "Exercise").

Dialogue on the Path of Initiation recounts a long conversation between Dürckheim and Alphonse Goettmann, a French Orthodox priest. At the beginning of the "Translator's Note" (by Nottingham) we read, "[Dürckheim] refers to 'Being' and 'God' interchangeably so as to avoid preconceived notions"(xi). A little later, we will look at the notion of God that emerges in his writings. For now, let us pay attention to the great significance of the first chapter of this book, which is a kind of spiritual and intellectual biography of Dürckheim. It is particularly noteworthy that, when confronted by death, Dürckheim discovered and received "life that is beyond life and death, LIFE in capitals..." (8; see also 65–67). He calls this type of arresting discovery "experience of Being." He also cites another very intense personal experience, which occurred while he was reading a passage by Lao Tzu (10-11). The insight that came to him seems to stem from an intuition of the contingency of things: since it is in contrast to empty space that a form or shape is identified, nothing exists, or functions, or is seen except projected against empty space. Whatever exists is made visible only against the backdrop of the invisible. Whether we look at this experience or the one that he had upon encountering death, or whether we look at other experiences confided to Dürckheim by his patients (see 59–61 and 106–107; also *Twofold*, 60–63), Dürckheim shows us the important role they play as points of entry to the divine.

Two levels of human consciousness

This vivid experience of Being allows Dürckheim to distinguish very clearly the two levels of human consciousness. The first level is that of the existential self, which constitutes that part of the human being that knows things in an analytical fashion by breaking down various objects and separating out ideas from each other; it is also the source of morally responsible behaviour. Dürckheim values this rational aspect and shows it to be necessary as a centre for control and creativity in the world. Alongside this existential self, he places the second level of human consciousness, the realm of Essential Being, in which one surrenders to the silent action of Being.

Understood in the light of Jung's distinction between the ego and the self (see *Dialogue*, 16), this duality corresponds roughly to two very different kinds of consciousness. However, I regret the fact that in praising the consciousness of Essential Being, Dürckheim fails to note the richness that may at times be present in the existential self. The existential self that he describes is a diminished one (see *Dialogue*, 66: the "self that has hardened"). Dürckheim describes the normal Western self whose method of knowing focuses on ideas rather than on questions and meaning to be discovered, and whose approach to morality is legalistic or gregarious, rather than based on values to be perceived, evaluated, and upheld with all one's strength. Dürckheim attributes to the existential self both an inferior mode of operation and a very noble one. He tends to transfer to the consciousness of Essential Being very attractive characteristics that I find belong to the existential self: for example, the sincere and active search for values, a sense of freedom in the face of group pressure, and the deepening of an interpersonal relationship (*Twofold*, 119–121; 176). While this dualistic way of presenting the human being corresponds to what is in fact our lived experience in contemporary culture, I would have preferred for him to have an anthropological vision that would show that the existential self, at its best, is open to transcendence.

Dürckheim nevertheless does a very great service: his emphasis on the duality of human life cautions us against the temptation to imagine Essential Being as psychological and corporeal awareness, brought about through sense perception. He invites us, on the contrary, to go through three stages of spiritual awakening. The first stage is based on a comment by Suzuki, the great Japanese Zen master: "Western knowledge looks outside, Eastern knowledge looks within." In relation to what Dürckheim has identified as the second stage, Suzuki adds: "But if you look within the way you look without, you make of the within a without." At a third stage, Dürckheim himself adds this extension: "Learn to look without the way you ought to look within." (*Dialogue*, 23).

Criteria of authenticity

Dürckheim shows himself to be a true spiritual master in his criteria of authenticity for the experience of Being. He begins by mentioning the "three great distresses" that "eat up" the human being: fear of death, destruction and annihilation; despair in the face of the absurdity and meaninglessness of life; and the utter sadness that comes from loneliness. He goes on to show that there are superficial and illusionary solutions to these three fundamental problems. We make efforts to obtain personal and material security, to give a degree of meaning to our projects and achievements, and to connect with a few people able to make us feel less lonely. These false solutions come from the natural self, that is, from a level of consciousness below that of Being.

The first criterion for discerning a true experience of Being consists of being liberated from the three basic distresses. In describing a person thus transformed, Dürckheim says, "he is no longer afraid of death, ...accepts meaninglessness and feels sheltered from solitude" (*Dialogue*, 67; see 67–68). He also says, "to no longer fear death—to see a meaning that is beyond the meaning and the non-meaning of this world—to live in a love that no longer depends in any way on sympathetic or unsympathetic feelings: these are the signs by which an other-worldly wisdom may be recognized" (*Twofold*, 66; see 66–71; this first criterion in *Dialogue* is used again in the third criterion in *Twofold*, 82–85). Is Dürckheim's way of putting it too blunt? Personally, I think it is a matter of experiencing a force so different that it makes the concern for personal security, the quest for a degree of meaning, and the search for human solidarity all totally relative. This criterion is really worth emphasizing since, very often, Christians speak of an immortality, a resurrection, a meaning of life, and a love that would appear to be more an extension of what this world can offer than access to an entirely new dimension.

What Dürckheim says too briefly of the second criterion in *Dialogue* (68) seems to correspond to the second criterion described at length in *Twofold* (78–82). He speaks here of the radiance, that expression of Being that shows through in the gaze, the attitudes, and the personality of the human being who is conscious of Transcendence. He carefully distinguishes this radiance from the radiance of youth, which we see in those still unaware of life's hardship, and from two forms of negative radiance: that of the darkness, that is, of a transcendent destructive force, and the false radiance—superficially attractive but cold and distant under the surface—of people whose deceiving egos, eager for power and prestige, have usurped the place of Essential Being.

The third criterion in *Dialogue* (68), which corresponds to the first in *Twofold* (75–78), is numinousness. Dürckheim uses this word coined by Rudolf Otto and based on the Latin word *numen* (power, divine greatness) to designate a sense of the presence of the "totally other" (the holy, the sacred, the ineffable) in all things. One is thus attentive to the fact that, even in the tiniest detail, a beauty can shine forth that is not of this world.

"The fourth criterion may be verified by the birth of a new consciousness" (*Dialogue*, 68; see *Twofold*, 85–86). One transcends the level of instinctive needs and guilt as the level of well as the level of communal solidarity. One becomes critical of these two levels, because of what is required by a higher authority, that of Essential Being. It is possible to live this critical consciousness on the level of the existential self at its best; on the other hand, this existential self may be strengthened by freedom of a religious nature. It is on that religious level that I would situate the replies of the apostles Peter and John, when they were asked by the Jewish authorities not to spread the message of Jesus: "Whether it is right in God's sight to listen to you rather than to God, you must judge; for we cannot keep from speaking about what we have seen and heard" (Acts 4:19-20).

The fifth criterion has to do with the intervention of the Enemy, the Adversary, the Devil. Every time human beings truly open themselves to the divine, a force makes itself felt which tries mightily to intimidate and discourage them and influence them in such a way that they do not make a resolved commitment in their Essential Being. "This is not a pious story, but a fact found in an inexplicable psychological experience" (*Dialogue*, 69; see *Our Twofold*, 86-87). Dürckheim connects the psychologically inexplicable nature of this phenomenon with the fact that the shock leading to the discouragement is brought on by an external event such as an attack or insult, an injury, some bad news, or an accident. Among contemporary Western youth open to the experience of Being, drugs are the easy temptation suggested by the Enemy. Even though the personal nature of this Enemy may be questioned, it remains true nevertheless that the demonic dimension is very real in the spiritual life. It is the inclination to refuse what is offered, to take only what suits us; this is what leads to our religious demise, this is how we lose our way.

Dürckheim and Christianity

Having presented what I have learned from Dürckheim, I would now like to explore the question of the extent to which his doctrine is Christian. I do so as a believer and a Catholic theologian who is trying both to listen to a spiritual master and to remain intellectually critical. My possible disagreement with certain aspects of his thought does not in any way imply that Dürckheim is less wise or less holy than I or than other Christians.

It is interesting to read the short testimony given by Alphonse Goettmann in his Introduction to *Dialogue on the Path of Initiation*. For Goettmann, who was born in the Catholic Church and became a priest in the Orthodox Church of France, Dürckheim was "'THE' master who made it possible to discover the only true Master, Jesus Christ!" (xiii; the emphasis on "the" is Goettmann's). I am not certain Dürckheim would agree to saying that Jesus Christ is "the only Master." In fact, he clearly places himself on the side of a common experience shared by various religions: "The experience of BEING is the star around which the spiritual life of all religions revolves. Whatever name it is given and whatever specific images are associated with it by the canons of the spiritual or religious traditions, with varying degrees of depth, persistence, or nuance, the core will always be the same, whether it is called Satori, Samadhi or Presentia Dei. Always and everywhere the experience exists" (*Twofold*, 89). Several religion experts reject this idea of a common core. For my part, however, I agree with Dürckheim that the experiential core is the same. The problem is knowing how to interpret it.

Dürckheim's easy alliance of Christian vocabulary with psychological, phenomenological, and philosophical vocabulary can give the illusion that his doctrine is entirely Christian. But we have only to note the difference in language between Goettmann (explicitly Christian) and Dürckheim (who retains from the Christian tradition what agrees with his own religious experience; see, for example, his interpretation of Jesus' "I am," *Dialogue*, 24 and 34) to question whether Dürckheim's thought can be classified as Christian. Goettmann himself does not seem to have wondered about this point, undoubtedly because he received so much from Dürckheim. I share a similar gratitude towards spiritual masters whose doctrine is not specifically Christian but who enabled me to rediscover in a startling way the transcendent dimension of life, and who enabled me to recognize treasures in my own Judeo-Christian tradition that had until then remained deeply buried. In contrast to Goettmann, however, I had found very early on in the Catholic world an authentic initiation to the living God. But like Goettmann, I often felt very much an outsider with many of my Catholic brothers and sisters, in whom I did not perceive a sense of the sacred and of transcendence. And so, very often, it was thanks to Protestants (Schleiermacher, James, and Otto), Jewish authors (Buber, Heschel, and Frankl), as well as Eastern mystics that my vacillating openness to God was maintained and confirmed.

Jacques Breton also acknowledges the debt that he, a committed Christian, owes to Dürckheim in his essay "L'expérience transcendentale."[16] Breton not only provides an excellent introduction to Dürckheim and his thought, he also takes the liberty of asking a few critical questions about him. Breton's appreciation of Dürckheim does not prevent him from noting that, although it is based on breathing, the Jesus Prayer of the Orthodox tradition—probably the closest form of Christian prayer to that practised by Dürckheim—nevertheless includes language and is addressed to a personal God who also speaks to the believer (Dürckheim replies to this objection in *Twofold*, 193–194). For Meister Eckhart, for the author of *The Cloud of Unknowing*, and for John of the Cross, "unknowing" God does not lead them to dismiss the personal character of God, as Dürckheim does.

Dürckheim points out the problem of the Catholic Church's tendency to condemn as heretical, spiritual teachers like Meister Eckhart. He complains that a Jesuit completely misunderstood him and unjustly attacked him (see *Dialogue*, 12). The short paragraph in which Dürckheim evokes this little controversy does not allow me to determine the extent of the misunderstanding that was involved. Even if church authorities have sometimes been unsympathetic or closed-minded towards the evocative and non-technical language of many spiritual teachers, it nevertheless remains their responsibility to determine whether the vast array of spiritualities that arise in every era are compatible with Christianity.

Another factor that makes it difficult to dialogue on this subject is Dürckheim's rather vague terminology, which is simultaneously psychological, philosophical, and Christian. Dürckheim does not believe in the usefulness of a technical vocabulary for transcendence. For him, the value of a language that defines reality is limited to the fields of science and action, which he sees as areas of ordering and manipulating data. In general, then, Dürckheim's aim is not so much to be precise as to evoke through suggestion the level where so-called supernatural experiences take place and to emphasize the contrast between this level and that of so-called natural consciousness. In my opinion, Dürckheim is at his best when he evokes fundamental experiences and demonstrates their fruitfulness. On the other, hand, when he interprets them with a little more philosophical precision, he outlines a position that is debatable and which I would like to try to identify.

Is God personal or impersonal?

To draw attention to our celestial origin, Dürckheim stresses the affinity that the part discovers between itself and the Whole. As long as the part feels distinct and separate from the Whole, it remains on the level of its natural consciousness and does not perceive this deep affinity. It only attains supernatural consciousness in the moment when, like a wave in the sea, it senses "the living truth that the sea is not just 'there', objectively present in front of it, across from it, but is contained in the vision of an internalized consciousness. Then, the wave will have not an objective awareness, but an intimate awareness, of being the sea" (*Twofold*, 25).

Dürckheim evokes here an experience that is both aesthetic and religious. He evokes an experience that is essential if one is to have access to a Reality that cannot be reduced to a god who is too personalized, a god who could be situated objectively in a specific place. We must be grateful to Dürckheim for repeatedly indicating clearly the type of consciousness that offers a window onto this incomparable Reality. However, it seems to me that Dürckheim lapses into a philosophical error when he interprets this experience of transcendence.

He claims that the basic discovery consists of "recognizing that one is part of the Whole and that one even is the Whole after the manner of the part" (*Twofold*, 25). He complements his metaphor of the wave with that of the vine branch: he insists, "The vine branch might realize one day, that deep down, it is the vine, in its branch-like way, that it is at home in the vine and that its true being, the root of its form, is the vine, that is to say, the whole of which it is a part." (*Twofold*, 26; the emphatic is is Dürckheim's).

What should we make of this bold statement? One encounters it just about everywhere in the writings of the mystics, including certain Christian mystics. Making a distinction between the experiences and their interpretations would help clarify things here. What are actually lived are experiences of transcendence; what is observed is that these experiences have an intuitive core through which one perceives a dimension that absolutely surpasses the human. But this core, which in principle can be distinguished from its interpretation, never exists in its pure state: as soon as one thinks and talks about it, it is characterized by images and words which constitute an interpretation. We can therefore recognize in the works of spiritual authors a similar experiential core variously interpreted. The basic experience lays the foundations for meditation and religion; without it, we would not even know what the religious traditions are talking about. On the other hand, there are times when spiritual authors are mistaken in their interpretations.

While I acknowledge as completely authentic the experiential core that Dürckheim evokes, I wonder about the way he interprets it when he states, not without clarity or emphasis, that the part is the Whole, after the manner of the part. What is this Whole? Unlike Dürckheim, who would no doubt say that human language is inadequate to answer this question, I believe it is useful to ask oneself whether this Whole is the universe (considered as infinite) or rather God (considered as a personal Infinite, different from the universe). On the one hand, the universe could not be this infinite Whole, because the universe is made up of limited and disparate parts, the entirety of which, being as limited as the sum of its parts, could never constitute an infinite Whole. On the other hand, the personal infinite Being, whom I call God, is this Whole from which every creature takes its origin without strictly being a part thereof.

I understand that for some readers, the considerations I am setting forth will appear abstract, inappropriate, or perhaps irrelevant. That may be because I am here going against a dogma of contemporary society, according to which interpretations of experience and life are not up for discussion. I believe, however, that they are, because a healthy human mind can always ask itself the question, "Is this interpretation correct?" It is a question about truth. It is legitimate to raise this question with respect to Dürckheim's writings, given that three very different interpretations of religious experience are involved here: one with a pantheistic orientation, one with a personalistic orientation, and the last with a supra-personalistic orientation.

The strength of the pantheistic orientation—where the Reality that one is conscious of is the Whole that the part is—is the way the human imagination functions. It cannot picture the world as being finite: even when it tries to place limits on the world, it imagines some place that is beyond these limits. In its spontaneous representation of the world as infinite, the imagination is nevertheless very useful to us. Indeed, the imagination opens up our feelings, heart, and intelligence to be able to perceive that which is absolutely beyond us. But when the intelligence claims that what the imagination has opened it up to is the Whole of which one *is* a part, it is going beyond the core of its experience and falls into error, for the universe is not in fact infinite (for the reason I have given above).

Let us move on now to the second interpretation. This is a naïve and personalistic vision of God. This God is imagined as a person (or three persons), alongside or above humanity. Dürckheim rightly rejects this naïve personalism, which proves incapable of incorporating the mode of consciousness that characterizes transcendental experience, where the Reality glimpsed does not appear as separate, that is, as a spatial object that can be imagined and conceptualized. It is obvious that, insofar as many Christians imagine God this way, even while often expressing their dissatisfaction with this image, they have something major to learn from Dürckheim.

However, both Dürckheim's language, with its pantheistic leaning, and naïve personalism remain unsatisfactory in the eyes of people who take the question of truth seriously and who hope to find answers. That is why we must consider a third interpretation of transcendental experience. According to this interpretation, that experience does not consist of perceiving that the part is the Whole, but of sensing an openness to the Whole and an affinity with the Whole. If the Whole is the origin of the part, and if the life of the Whole runs through the finite being that depends on it, then as the human self is a finite being, it cannot be the Whole; and the human self has such an affinity with the Whole that the Whole gives it its identity (this is a bit like saying Montreal gives Montrealers their identity). "In him we live and move and have our being.... For we too are his offspring" (Acts 17:28). Our participation in the divine life does not stem from the human self being God after the manner of the part. Rooted in the affinity between the human self and God, our participation in the divine life is pure gift from God, which he freely wills and offers.

Despite these differences between Dürckheim's doctrine and Christianity, I find his practice and thought very close to Christianity. Moreover, he sees the unity between East and West in Christianity, because of the synthesis it makes between interiority and exteriority (*Twofold*, 20 and 93). For Christians and non-Christians alike, reading Dürckheim's writings will bring enlightened consciousness and enhance their lives.

13

Bernard Lonergan:
A Theologian in Dialogue

C anadian Jesuit Bernard Lonergan has much to offer to those who are dedicated to the intellectual journey and sharing of questions and discoveries. Not only is he widely considered to be one of the greatest theologians of the twentieth century, but he was also an unparalleled seeker in dialogue. Lonergan was born to Irish-Canadian parents at Buckingham, Quebec, in 1904; during the course of his life he taught in Montreal, Toronto, Rome, and Boston; he died in Toronto in 1984.

First discoveries

Lonergan received a traditional Catholic upbringing. However, he was also part of a generation—that of Congar and Rahner, also born in 1904—keen to innovate with a mixture of boldness and caution. His thinking first took him towards rediscovering the vitality of Thomas Aquinas, in a personal and engaging manner, working through the crust of a certain rigid and ahistorical Thomism.[17] In reaction against a philosophical tradition which he traces from Duns Scotus to Neo-scholasticism, and which he accuses of being conceptualist, Lonergan advocates an "intellectualist" approach: what matters, he claims, is not a store of concepts to be accumulated, but a lively intelligence that can synthesize a body of data and formulate an illuminating hypothesis on a subject.

Lonergan's second outstanding contribution flows from this "intellectualism." He had a passion for mathematics, the natural sciences, and economics. In his book *Insight: A Study of Human Understanding*,[18] he sets out to establish a connection between Aristotelian and Thomistic philosophy on the one hand and contemporary science on the other. Unlike many other writers, he does not establish this connection according to a framework of themes—that would be a conceptualist approach—but according to what he calls the intellectualist approach: a framework of the operations that the human mind engages in when it works scientifically. Lonergan subsequently extends his epistemological interest to the human sciences and history (see especially Chapters 3, 8, and 9 of *Method in Theology*, MT in the references to follow).

Lonergan's intellectualist approach, from the late 1950s onward—without diminishing its achievements to that point—nevertheless broadens and becomes part of the more comprehensive context of the pursuit of values through action. He states that the concerns of his students, both at the Gregorian University in Rome and at the summer seminars he held in Canada and the United States have contributed to his evolution. He realizes that the culture and society in which these young people live are characterized by existentialism, with its emphasis on freedom, decision-making, and commitment. Lectures entitled *"Existenz* and *Aggiornamento"*[19] and "Dimensions of Meaning" testify to this awareness.

The importance of meaning

A few years later, Lonergan revisits the importance of meaning in human life. When he presents meaning as being incarnate in symbol, he covers a vast territory shared by art, psychology and religion (see MT, Ch. 3). Defined as "an image of a real or imaginary object that evokes a feeling or is evoked by a feeling" (MT, 64), the symbol establishes connections—of harmony or discord—between the psyche, which reacts to images and feelings, and the intentional consciousness, which tries to evaluate the realities perceived. It plays a pivotal role in a person's internal communication. Faced with the problem of this harmony and this communication, Lonergan situates the contribution of the various kinds of psychotherapy in an interesting way. He indicates the diversity of interpretative contexts to which therapeutic practices belong. Theologians need not accept these passively without saying a word, but should identify and discuss the philosophical prerequisites that condition them. Robert Doran, a Lonergan disciple who lives in Toronto and has studied Jungian thought in depth, has creatively extended this openness of theology to psychology. He developed the concept of psychic conversion, and thus created a space where theology, spirituality, and psychology can meet and unite their efforts to elucidate an important side of human growth.[20]

Meaning is found at the heart of a specific culture: "Culture is the meaning of a way of life."[21] This meaning is created and communicated in a complex manner and is refined in intersubjective relationships, attitudes and gestures, words and silences, projects and achievements, institutions, dreams, works of art, and writings. Contrary to what the classicist notion of culture meant for many people in the modern era, it is not really possible to speak of "culture" in the universal and normative sense, with its immutable ideals and models.[22] In contrast to this classicist understanding of culture, there is an empirical understanding, which is characterized by the infinite sets of meanings analyzed by the human sciences. For Lonergan, the great challenge of adapting to the contemporary world the Catholic Church faces consists of making the difficult transition from a classicist view of culture, religion, and theology to an empirical view.[23] Not without humour, he adds, "This is a matter involved in considerable confusion. The confusion arises mainly because classicist culture made no provision for the possibility of its own demise."[24] One can guess the divergent consequences that these two notions of culture entail for dialogue. A man of classicist culture like Bossuet, for example, despite his great sincerity, must remain unbending with respect to Leibniz's propositions on ecumenism.[25] One might also wonder whether the sterility of the religious controversies of the seventeenth and eighteenth centuries is due in large part to the confrontation between the classicist and empirical notions of truth.

In the nineteenth and twentieth centuries, another antithesis concerning culture becomes established among historians and those in the human sciences. In one camp are found the positivists and behaviorists who consider the human being only as a superior animal; in the other are those who place the quest for meaning and the search for values at the heart of living.[26] Lonergan claims that a reductionist attitude reduces living to its biological, zoological, and psychological characteristics and does not take sufficient account of the specific properties of intentionality, that is to say, our ability to aim for, if not always to achieve, an intelligent commitment. This reductionism introduces distortions both in our image of the human person and in the hypotheses and concepts used in the human sciences. There is room here for a dialectic whose practice signals "the end of the age of innocence, the age that assumed that human authenticity could be taken for granted."[27] Lonergan believes that authenticity depends in large part on what vision one has of the human being and human behaviour. That being the case, a true dialogue would not be able to eliminate these divergencies. The attitude of mind that Lonergan proposes is profoundly different from other Christian thinkers who state categorically that one must accept *the* contemporary psychology or sociology, without recognizing the incompatibilities that exist both within these disciplines and between some of their assumptions and those of the Christian faith. On the other hand, he does not put religious experience or church doctrines on a pedestal either, for these too can be contaminated by inauthenticity. This is to say that the invitation to be transformed through dialogue on the intellectual, moral, and religious levels is addressed to everyone.[28]

A subjectivity that is open to the Other

Given the emphasis that Lonergan's theology places on the knowing and acting subject, the psychic life of that subject, the diversity of the webs of cultural meaning which that subject has been part of over time, the contradictory interpretations of the person, personal experience and personal possibility, we can say that it fosters a dialogue that truly is knowledge—either direct or historical—of others. However, one can wonder how such awareness of otherness and of historicity would not bring about a certain relativism with respect to truth. This is the fundamental problem—which Lonergan has not evaded, for his life's work has been precisely to develop a philosophy and a methodology that would justify subjectivity as well as objectivity. For Lonergan, objective truth is reached when the human subject applies all their potential: psyche, intelligence, freedom. Clearly there will always remain dark and light areas, for the knowledge and action of every person and every society includes a mixture of absurdity and intelligence. The challenge is, therefore, to find criteria that will enable us to distinguish error from truth, distortion from wholeness, and unauthenticity from authenticity.

This chapter is not the place to present these criteria, which are very complex (and which an assiduous reader will be able to follow in MT, especially in Chapters 4, 11 and 12). I shall therefore only indicate the main line of reasoning that permits Lonergan to believe that a Christian can at the same time be fully subjective and fully objective in receiving and appropriating the word of God. It is a matter of distinguishing between religious experience and the word, or between faith and belief. On the one hand, religious experience, understood as "the experience of being in love with God," and faith, defined as "the knowledge born of religious love," constitute the summit of the subjective life. On the other hand, the word handed down by a tradition gives meaning to religious experience by situating it in a world of meanings; as for beliefs, they express the value judgments made by a faith that discerns the importance of what a religious tradition offers. Thus, word and belief direct us towards an objectivity suggested by those other than ourselves and, ultimately, by God (see MT 105–119).

In other words, human intentionality tries to go beyond itself in openness to realities that it observes, understands, verifies, honours and loves. This openness may be directed towards a Mysterious Other with whom one perceives one is nevertheless in love despite all one's personal weaknesses. Although this inclination to open oneself to others and to the Mysterious Other is transcultural, it is only acted upon and carried out from within a particular culture. While religious beliefs offer guidance for discovering the meaning of our more or less successful openness to others and to the Mysterious Other, in today's world it is individual cultures that transmit these religious beliefs. The noblest exercise of human responsibility, the one which confers on it its greatest dignity, consists of responding positively to the transcultural requirement, embodied in a culture, to love others and the Mysterious Other with a deep love, and to accept the truth of that love. When this thirst to love and acknowledge others and the Mysterious Other encounters the Judeo-Christian tradition, which asserts that it carries within it the self-revelation of God, human responsibility identifies the possibility of its most engaging decision. It is such a decision, grounded in seeking and evaluating, and motivated by intelligence and love, that gives us access (even if this access has obscure areas) to objective truth, while at the same time we remain on a subjective course.

This way of presenting subjectivity and objectivity shows the complementarity between seeking and religious discovery. It also lets us establish the conditions of authenticity necessary for fruitful interaction between our faith and our commitment in the world. Both faith and commitment can be either full of vitality or severely handicapped. Lonergan's thought can therefore help us to get beyond the absolute language of principles and "in itself" statements, and to adopt the empirical language of the human sciences expressed in formulas like "everything depends on the factors involved." A theology thus understood remains normative—as, moreover, does much in the human sciences—but in a manner that is far more flexible and nuanced than classical theology.

While reading the works of Lonergan may prove to be a demanding task, it nevertheless provides a philosophical, theological, and methodological framework that easily handles the questions asked by people who are searching and who are influenced by history, the sciences, and the great issues facing the world today. The solutions outlined are presented at a basic level. That is the particular way that Lonergan wished, throughout his intellectual journey, to honour the noblest aspect of the human being.[29]

Conclusion

The theology that inspired this book emphasizes the intellectual, psychological, moral, and religious dynamics at work in society and in the churches. It also, but secondarily, looks at factors that dull the authenticity of faith. This accent on the positive is a way of honouring the original goodness of the human being as well as the action of the Holy Spirit, which makes itself felt daily in our lives. This vision is, however, more than mere optimism, for it stems from Christian hope, a hope which therefore allows us to give prominence to the desire to find an ultimate meaning to our personal and collective existence; to our search for fulfillment, love and communion; to the concern to integrate one's personality and one's actions with respect to both ideas and emotions; to honesty in the face of problems of a cognitive as well as a practical nature, honesty in accepting the incomplete character of our positions and in being open to the perspectives of others; to respect for the intelligence and freedom of each person, whatever challenges they may face; to suffering without resignation in the face of the miseries and injustices experienced in our world; to infinite gratitude towards God for his creative act renewed each day, for the revelation by which God makes himself known, for the free gift of his loving presence and for what he offers and accomplishes in the church.

These forces constitute an existential whole. In this book I have tried to stress the fact that the components of Christian experience form a coherent whole. My purpose in describing the various parts has been, in each case, to better explain how they function—sometimes in harmony and sometimes in tension—in everyday life. I can only hope that, through this process, you have been able to identify and clarify your own personal discoveries and to forge new paths.

Notes

1   Or, rather, the external unanimity (sometimes even interrupted) that character-
     ized the ultramontane period from about 1870 to 1960 and represents a brief
     exception in church history.

2   Paul Ricoeur, *Freud and Philosophy: An Essay on Interpretation*, trans. Denis Savage
     (New Haven, CT: Yale University Press, 1970), 28.

3   My description of the five levels of intentionality closely follows Bernard Lon-
     ergan, *Method in Theology* (Toronto: University of Toronto Press, 1992), 4–25,
     30–41, 101–107. However, it was only after having written this book, first pub-
     lished in 1972, that Lonergan adumbrated a distinction between the fourth and
     fifth levels. See Frederick E. Crowe, "An Exploration of Lonergan's New Notion
     of Value," in *Appropriating the Lonergan Idea*, ed. Michael Vertin (Washington, DC:
     The Catholic University of America Press, 1989), 51–70.

4   *Turning East: The Promise and Peril of the New Orientalism* (New York: Simon and
     Schuster, 1977).

5   M. Eliade, cited by H. Cox, *Turning East*, 103.

6   New York: The Free Press, 1973.

7   New York: Rinehart, 1947.

8   *The Psychological Birth of the Human Infant* (New York: Basic Books, 1975).

9   *The Crucified Jesus Is No Stranger*, ix.

10   See, for example, A.H. Maslow, *Toward a Psychology of Being* (2nd ed., New York:
     Van Nostrand, 1968) and K.G. Dürckheim (see my Chapter 12).

11   These remarks are based on Antoine Vergote, *The Religious Man: A Psychological
     Study of Religious Attitudes*, trans. Marie-Bernard Saïd (Dublin: Gill and Macmillan,
     1969), and *Interprétation du langage religieux* (Paris: Seuil, 1974).

12   Think of the evolution of a monk such as Thomas Merton: see H.J.M. Nouwen,
     Pray to Live (Notre Dame, IN: Fides, 1972).

13   Montréal: Editions du Méridien, 1984.

14   See comments made by Robert Vachon and Kalpana Das, cited and adopted by
     André Couture in: "Réincarnation et résurrection? Revue d'un débat et amorce
     d'une recherche," *Science et Esprit* 36 (1984): 367 and 372.

15   *Our Twofold Origin* (London: Allen & Unwin, 1983); *Dialogue on the Path of Initiation*
     (New York: Globe Press Books, 1991).

16   *Le Supplément* 123 (1977): 513–521.

[17] See his *Verbum: Word and Idea in Aquinas* (Toronto: University of Toronto Press, 1997).

[18] Toronto: University of Toronto Press, 1992.

[19] In *Collection* (Toronto: University of Toronto Press, 1988), 222–231 and 232–245.

[20] Robert M. Doran, *Psychic Conversion and Theological Foundations* (Chico, CA: Scholars Press), 1981.

[21] "The Absence of God in Modern Culture," in Bernard Lonergan, *A Second Collection* (Toronto: University of Toronto Press, 1996), 102.

[22] Ibid., 101.

[23] Ibid., 107–111; "The Future of Christianity," ibid., 159–161.

[24] Ibid., 160.

[25] See Paul Hazard, *The European Mind (1680–1715)*, trans. J. Lewis May (Cleveland: The World Publishing Company, 1967), part II, chap. 4: "Bossuet at Bay."

[26] "The Absence of God," *A Second Collection*, 104–106, and *Method in Theology*, 248–249.

[27] "The Ongoing Genesis of Methods," in Bernard Lonergan, *A Third Collection* (New York: Paulist Press, 1985): 156.

[28] See the three conversions in *Method in Theology*, 237–244.

[29] For another reflection on Lonergan's thought, see Louis Roy, "La contribution de Bernard Lonergan à la théologie contemporaine," *Studies in Religion /Sciences Religieuses*, 14 (1985): 475–485.